ON
THE STAGE
–AND OFF

'I thought that all acting was making love in tights to pretty women.'

ON
THE STAGE
–AND OFF

THE BRIEF CAREER OF
A WOULD-BE ACTOR

JEROME K. JEROME

With an Introduction by
Jeremy Nicholas

with One Hundred Illustrations by
Kenneth M. Skeaping

ALAN SUTTON

First published in this edition in the United Kingdom in 1991 by
Alan Sutton Publishing Limited · Phoenix Mill · Far Thrupp · Stroud · Gloucestershire

First published in the United States of America in 1991 by
Alan Sutton Publishing Inc · Wolfeboro Falls · NH 03896–0848

British Library Cataloguing in Publication Data

Jerome, Jerome K. (Jerome Klapka) *1859–1927*
On the stage – and off : the brief career of a would-be actor.
1. Theatre. England, history
I. Title
792.0942

ISBN 0-86299-886-7

Library of Congress Cataloging in Publication Data applied for

Photographs pages xiv, xvi, 5, 8, 12, 16, 21,
25, 30, 36, 42, 47, 52, 57, 63, 68, 74, 80, 84, 88, 92,
96, 100, 103, 108, 111, 115, 120, 126, 132 and 139
courtesy of The University of Bristol
Theatre Collection

Typeset in 10/14 Bembo
Typesetting and origination by
Alan Sutton Publishing Limited.
Printed in Great Britain by
The Bath Press, Bath, Avon.

· CONTENTS ·

· CONTENTS ·

by
Jeremy Nicholas

It all began with Henry Wadsworth Longfellow. At least, if it hadn't been for him, Jerome K. Jerome might never have written *On the Stage – and Off.* One evening in 1884, Jerome was sitting miserably by his fireside, impoverished, rejected by a string of publishers and editors, reading the poems of his current favourite. He came upon the opening lines of the curiously entitled 'Gaspar Becerra' from Longfellow's 'By the Fireside':

> By his evening fire the artist
> Pondered o'er his secret shame;
> Baffled, weary, and disheartened,
> Still he mused, and dreamed of fame.

It struck a chord. The last stanza convinced him that Longfellow was writing about his own case:

> O thou sculptor, painter, poet!
> Take this lesson to thy heart:
> That is best which lieth nearest;
> Shape from that thy work of art.

Of course! Give up the imaginary and fanciful tales which had met with so little success. Write about what he knew – the life of an itinerant actor. He had three years of adventures to tell. The idea seized him. It took him just three months to complete the task.

★

An orphan at fifteen, Jerome had caught the acting bug while a clerk for the London and North Western Railway at Euston. The little extra money he earned from overtime was spent on visits to the theatre, and a young friend of his had left his humble job in the city and gone on the stage. He was quickly hooked. But then, as he observes in the opening sentence of the book, 'There comes a time in everyone's life when he feels he was born to be an actor. Something within him tells him that he is the coming man, and that one day he will electrify the world . . . This sort of thing generally takes a man when he is about nineteen, and lasts till he is nearly twenty.'

Jerome made his professional debut at the age of eighteen (under the name of Harold Crichton) and for the next three years alternately revelled in and despaired of the life whose 'glorious uncertainty . . . almost rivals that of the turf'.

Three years was enough. 'Though I say so myself, I think I would have made a good actor,' he wrote in *My Life and Times*, his autobiography published in 1926, the year before his death at the age of sixty-eight. 'Could I have lived on laughter and applause, I would have gone on. I certainly got plenty of experience. I have played every part in *Hamlet* except Ophelia. I have doubled the parts of Sairey Gamp and Martin Chuzzlewit on the same evening. I forget how the end came. I remember selling my wardrobe in some town up north, and reaching London with thirty shillings in my pocket. . . . Fortunately the weather was mild and I was used to "sleeping rough".'

Fame and fortune as a performer might have eluded him, but thereafter Jerome and the theatre never parted company. Now in his early twenties, Jerome found himself at the bottom of the social pile. He bumped into a childhood friend who had also 'fallen upon evil days, and had taken to journalism'. Jerome followed suit and became a penny-a-liner, selling to newspapers whatever stories he could cover by dashing all over London. His copy was paid at the rate of (to be accurate) three-halfpence a line. Abandoning that cutthroat world he tried school-mastering in Clapham, then became in turn secretary to an illiterate north London builder, buyer and packer for a firm of commission agents, and worked for a firm of parliamentary agents (today's professional lobbyists).

Throughout this period he read voraciously and wrote copiously – stories, plays, essays, satires – for he knew, despite his meanderings, that he must be a writer. Only one effort was rewarded with publication, in a paper called *The Lamp*. 'It died,' Jerome recalled, 'soon afterwards.'

Longfellow's poem provided timely inspiration. It both encouraged him to change direction and showed him the new path he should follow. At the time of writing *On the Stage – and Off* Jerome had slid into yet another job, as a solicitor's clerk with vague thoughts of training for the law. He had lodgings in a second-floor room at the back of a house in Whitfield Street, off Tottenham Court Road in London, which enjoyed a view of an extensive burial ground:

· INTRODUCTION ·

For a workroom I often preferred the dark streets to my dismal bed-sitting room. Portland Place was my favourite study. I liked its spacious dignity. With my note-book and a pencil in my hand, I would pause beneath each lamp-post and jot down the sentence I had just thought out. At first the police were suspicious. I had to explain to them. Later they got friendly; and often I would read to them some passage I thought interesting or amusing. There was an Inspector – a dry old Scotchman who always reached Langham church as the clock struck eleven: he was the most difficult. Whenever I made him laugh, I went home feeling I had done good work.

Shortly after the book was finished, Jerome left his graveside panorama and moved round the corner to a front room at 36 Newman Street. In a back room in the same building lived a similarly impecunious young man, a bank clerk named George Wingrave. The landlady suggested that it might be more economical for them to share one room between them and this they did, quickly becoming firm friends. George and Jerome spent much of their spare time and money on visits to the theatre – a common passion, they found – and it was through these that they met another theatre-lover, Carl Hentschel, soon to be re-christened William Harris. All in all, the theatre was exercising a remarkable influence on Jerome's life, on the stage – and off.

★

Re-reading *On the Stage – and Off* reminded me how good it is as social history. If nothing else, it provides a remarkably vivid and useful source on life in the theatre of the 1880s. It tells how the whole game worked, how it was set up and what a dog's life it was. The inhabitants of these sketches – there is no real story line as such – live in the shadows of their glamorous, highly-paid West End colleagues. A glimpse of the London suburban theatres is the most to which Jerome's over-worked, ill-treated second- and third-raters can hope to aspire, surviving, as they do, on broken contracts and pathetic optimism. It is an under-documented area of stage history and as such is valuable.

But, of course, it is a lot more than that. In the brief period that he trod the boards, Jerome came to know the theatre and actors very well. He got inside the business (not an easy thing to do). What I had forgotten was just how amusing the book is and, which struck me most forcibly, what similarities there are with life in the provincial theatre of the 1990s. The delights and disappointments Jerome experienced will exact a

· INTRODUCTION ·

groan of despairing recognition and a chortle of shared joy from every Equity member in the land. It should be required reading at all drama colleges *pour encourager les autres*.

Nothing very much has changed. The ridiculously low wages in the theatre remain a scandal; Jerome swipes at crooked managers, overweening minor stars and grasping agents, and wonders if the latter – 'these meddlers on commission' – will ever be stamped out. There was certainly a larger number of unscrupulous managers around in Jerome's day, but the back page of today's *Equity Journal* (headed in time-honoured fashion 'For Your Special Attention'), contains a surprisingly long list of organisations and individuals with whom one is forbidden or advised not to work.

'Where To Stay' is still top of the agenda when one lands a tour (far more urgent than learning lines) and exercises the ingenuity and enterprise of every artist. Landlady stories are legion and Jerome does not let us down. (I shall never forget a friend of mine reporting on the ghastly taste in interior decor of one such member of the species who appeared to have a fur lampshade in her dining-room. On reaching up to stroke it to see if it was real, the 'fur' came off at his touch. It was dust – perfectly layered, half-an-inch thick.)

Dressing-rooms too, a century on, are forever the subject of comment and concern. They may have basins and mirrors nowadays but they do not often have windows; if they do, there will be no heating and the door will not lock; if the door does lock, there will be neither basin nor mirror. Dressing-rooms and back-stage amenities are designed, generally, to make life uncomfortable for the actor, the theory being that the more uncomfortable he is, the better job he will do. (Actors are traditionally the only people never to be consulted when a new theatre is built.) But, who knows, if we were suddenly to be given everything and live the cosseted, glamorous existence that the public imagines we do, we might lose our edge and our reputation for producing the finest actors in the world.

Jerome's career as a 'would-be actor' may have been brief, but it was also intense. Any thespian worth his salt reading these snatches of autobiography today will recognize a fellow pro. by his authentic tone – a tone that can only be acquired, never adopted. The in-house bitching, the anxiety of finding the next week's rent and the next job (and, once you have it, moaning about it), the chatty amiability of the green room (the actors' communal rest room) – 'twas ever thus, it seems.

★

Jerome's adventures may provide us with a lively cast of late-Victorian mummers and their hand-to-mouth struggle for dignity and a decent meal; they provided Jerome with the raw material on which to cut his new-found teeth. Throughout the book are trial runs of passages echoed in his second book, *Idle Thoughts of an Idle Fellow*, and, especially, his fourth, *Three Men in a Boat*. (His third work, *Stage-Land*, again draws on his acting days and is a series of vignettes caricaturing the stock stage characters of the day – Hero, Comic Man, Irishman, Servant Girl, etc.) Thus, chapter seven of *On the Stage – and Off* ends with a bit of fun about there never being any green room:

> I met an old actor once who had actually been in one, and I used to get him to come and tell me all about it. But even his recollections were tinged with vagueness. He was not quite sure whether it had been at Liverpool or at Newcastle that he had come across it, and at other times he thought it must have been at Exeter. But wherever it was, the theatre had been burnt down a good many years ago – about that he was positive.

This is a rehearsal for the celebrated search for the eleven-five train from Waterloo in *Three Men in a Boat*. Similarly, the pathetic end of Mad Mat in chapter twelve – 'People who have lived for any length of time on six shillings a week don't take long to die when they set about it . . .' – is elaborated in *Three Men in a Boat* in the episode of the drowned woman at Goring: 'Six shillings a week does not keep body and soul together very unitedly. They want to get away from each other when there is only such a very slight bond as that between them.' The struggle with the travelling basket in chapter ten is a splendid forerunner of a recurring Jeromian theme – the bewildering life of inanimate objects.

On the Stage – and Off did not achieve instantaneous success. Several periodicals supplied him with the familiar rejection slips. Finally, a new publication came up trumps: *The Play* edited by a retired actor, Aylmer Gowing.

He was [remembered Jerome,] the first editor who up till then had seemed glad to see me when I entered the room. He held out both hands to me and offered me a cigarette. It all seemed like a dream. He told me that what he liked about my story was that it was true. He had been through it all himself, forty years before. He asked me what I wanted for the serial rights. I was only too willing to let him have them for nothing, upon which he shook hands with me again, and gave me a five pound note. It was the first time I had ever possessed a five pound note. . . . I could not bear the idea of spending it. I put it away at the bottom of an old tin box. . . . Later, when my luck began to turn, I fished it out, and with part of it . . . I purchased an old Georgian bureau which has been my desk ever since.

In 1885 Field and Tuer published the work in book form. Jerome had to make them a gift of the copyright for the privilege, but there it was, measuring 4 inches by 3 inches in a pink dust-jacket, even if the 'K' of the author's name was printed followed by a small 'j', so that many thought the author was called Jerome Kjerome. He later recalled:

> The book sold fairly well, but the critics were shocked. The majority denounced it as rubbish and, three years later, on reviewing my next book *Idle Thoughts of an Idle Fellow*, regretted that an author who had written such an excellent first book should have followed it up by so unworthy a successor. I think I may claim to have been, for the first twenty years of my career, the best abused author in England.

Jerome K. Jerome, however, with his first book, was on his way at last.

The following year, after the success of *Idle Thoughts*, Field and Tuer (now The Leadenhall Press) re-issued *On the Stage – and Off* in tobacco-brown hard covers with the addition of 'one hundred illustrations by Kenneth M. Skeaping'. Very good illustrations they are too, though neither Jerome in his autobiography nor any reference book I have come across make any mention of them.

By the time *Idle Thoughts* had been published, Jerome had already completed his first (one-act) play, *Barbara*. Three further plays appeared in 1888. His brief career on stage had also taught him the mechanics of playwriting. He wrote another ten plays (possibly more), a number of them making a bigger hit across the Atlantic than in England. Among these now forgotten offerings were a couple of farces – *Biarritz*, and *The MacHaggis*, in which the heroine not only rode a bicycle and smoked a cigarette on stage for the first time, but said 'Damn' *twice* in the last act, years before Mrs Patrick Campbell said 'Bloody'!

By far the most successful of his plays was *The Passing of the Third Floor Back*, first produced in 1908. It starred the great Sir Johnston Forbes-Robertson as the stranger who mysteriously changes the lives of the inhabitants of a seedy boarding-house. It is a morality play, devoid of any Jeromian glibness or wit, sentimental to the point of making its revival today unlikely, but it was performed constantly over the next two decades. I have a letter from Jerome to Frank Forbes-Robertson, Sir Johnston's son, giving the latter permission for another touring production in 1925 on terms of Jerome receiving 5 per cent of the gross takings.

Jerome's dramatic works have not stood the test of time, though (on a personal note) the unlikely proposition of a one-man stage version of *Three Men in a Boat* ran for four months in London's May Fair Theatre in the early 1980s. As I write, a brand new musical of the book is touring the country. Yet I suspect the fact that Jerome himself was ever connected to the theatre in any degree will be news to most people. That he was once a professional actor, that his three years in the theatre made him as a man and a writer, that his first book tells the story of his brief career and that it is written to a sparkling standard not so very far short of his most celebrated creation, might elicit the same reaction as the lady who, on one occasion, asked Jerome why he did not write for the theatre:

'I am sure, Mr Jerome,' she continued with a bright, encouraging smile, 'that you could write a play.'
I told her that I had written nine: that six of them had been produced, that three of them had been successful both in England and America, that one of them was still running at the Comedy Theatre and approaching its two hundredth night. Her eyebrows went up in amazement.
'Dear me,' she said, 'you do surprise me.'

BARLEY FEN
SEPTEMBER 1990

THE NEW DRAMA OF THE

Flying Dutchman, or The Phantom Ship

having on Monday Night excited the most lively Expressions of Astonishment and Admiration, on account of the Novel and Wonderful Machinery and Transformations which occur, and the Thrilling Effect it produced, will be repeated on *Wednesday* and *Friday* next.

On Wednesday Evening, March 7,

Will be presented, second time at this Theatre, a New, Nautical, Melo-Dramatic Play, called

The Flying
DUTCHMAN;
OR, THE
PHANTOM SHIP.

"THE FLYING DUTCHMAN" is said to be an Amsterdam Vessel, which about a Century ago sailed from that Port ;—the Masters's Name was *Vanderdecken*, whose constant Boast it was, that " he always would have his own Way, in spite of Fate."

Once, on doubling the Cape, they were a whole Day trying to weather *Table Bay*, the Wind increasing, a-head of them, and *Vanderdecken* walking the Deck, continued swearing fearfully—just after Sun-set, he was spoke by a Vessel, who asked him if he did not mean to go into the Bay that Night, to which *Vanderdecken*, with a tremendous Oath, replied, " he would not, though he should beat about till the Day of Judgment." *Vanderdecken* never did go into *Table Bay*, and is believed to undergo the Doom he so desperately dared. His Vessel is still seen in the *Cape Seas* in foul Weather, sailing against the fiercest Storm, with every Inch of Canvas set, striving in vain to reach her home, or to send Despatches to Relatives by other Vessels.—The hints upon which the Drama is founded, were taken from a short and interesting Article in *Blackwood's Magazine*, from whence also the above Account is extracted.

Leader of the Band, Mr. G. STANSBURY, in consequence of his Brother's severe Accident.

The New Overture and the whole of the Music composed by Mr. G. H. Rodwel.

The Dresses by Mr. and Miss Lewis.—The Scenery by Messrs. Donaldson, Carrol, & Assistants.
As performed and now performing at the Theatre-Royal, Adelphi, London, with Unprecedented Attraction, Admiration, and Applause.

Captain Peppercoat (formerly Captain of a Trade Ship) . Mr. DUFF | Lieut. Mowdrey .. Mr. BRINDAL
Tom Willis (Mate of the Enterprise).. Mr. HORSMAN | Sentinel.. Mr. MORTON
Mynheer Von Swiggs (Purser) .... Mr. MATTHEWS | Smutta (a Slave) .... Mr. ROSS
Peter Von Bummell (a Cockney Dutchman, a Dabbler in the Law).......... Mr. BAKER
Toby Varnish, his Friend (a Physical Marine Painter and a Bear).. Mr. GARTON
Vanderdecken (Captain of the Flying Dutchman).. Mr. HENRY
Sailors, Soldiers, Slaves, Spirits of the Deep, &c. &c.
Rockalda (an Evil Spirit of the Deep).............. Mr. ROE
Lestelle Vanhelm............Miss TAYLOR | Lucy .... Mrs. BRINDAL.

SUCCESSION OF THE SCENERY, &c.

Rockalda's Cavern—Mysterious Appearance of Vanderdecken

OAK CHAMBER IN FORTRESS, formerly belonging to Vanderdecken.

DECK OF THE ENTERPRISE.

SUN-SET, AT SEA.—Approach of

THE PHANTOM SHIP.
Haunted Chamber in the Fortress.
EXTERIOR OF THE FORTRESS.
Vanishing of VANDERDECKEN and LESTELLE.

RISING of the SEA-MIST.—The SCENE ENVELOPED in DARKNESS.—The

Phantom Ship in full sail,
ON THE OPEN SEA.   GIGANTIC CLIFF.
Inundation of *ROCKALDA's Cave.*

To conclude with the admired Farce of

SIMPSON & Co.
Or, No. 15, Harley-Street.

Mr. Simpson............Mr. BAKER
Mr. Bromly.........Mr. GARTON | Foster,..... Mr. ROE | Servant............Mr. WESTON
Mrs. Bromly,.... Miss GEORGE; being her second appearance on this Stage.
Mrs. Fitzallan................ Miss PITT | Madame La Trappe ....Mrs. FREDERICK
And, Mrs. Simpson........Mrs. M'CREADY.

On Friday Evening will be presented, third time, the New Musical Play of THE FLYING DUTCHMAN, or The Phantom Ship. To which will be added an entire New Melo-Dramatic Entertainment called LUKE THE LABOURER ; or, The Lost Son, interspersed with Songs, Glees, &c. &c. Written by J. B. Buckstone, Esq. As performed at the Theatre-Royal, Adelphi, and now performing there with Universal Approbation.

Tickets, and Places in the Boxes, to be had at the Theatre, from Eleven till Three o'clock.
Tickets for the Pit and Gallery to be had at the General Printing-Office, 9, Narrow Wine-Street.

SOMERTON, Printer.

In penning the following pages I have endeavoured to be truthful. In looking back upon the scenes through which I passed, I have sought to penetrate the veil of glamour Time trails behind him as he flies, and to see things exactly as they were – to see the rough road as well as the smiling landscape, the briers and brambles as well as the green grass and the waving trees.

Now, however, that my task is done, and duty no longer demands that memory should use a telescope, the mellowing haze of distance resumes its sway, and the Stage again appears the fair, enchanted ground that I once dreamt it. I forget the shadows, and remember but the brightness. The hardships that I suffered seem now but picturesque incidents; the worry only pleasurable excitement.

I think of the Stage as of a lost friend. I like to dwell upon its virtues and to ignore its faults. I wish to bury in oblivion the bad, bold villains and the false-hearted knaves who played a part thereon, and to think only of the gallant heroes, the virtuous maidens, and the good old men.

Let the bad pass. I met far more honest, kindly faces than deceitful ones, and I prefer to remember the former. Plenty of honest, kindly hands grasped mine, and such are the hands that I like to grip again in thought. Where the owners of those kindly hands and faces may be now I do not know. Years have passed since I last saw them, and the sea of life has drifted us farther and farther apart. But wherever on that sea they may be battling, I call to them from here a friendly greeting. Hoping that my voice may reach across the waves that roll between us, I shout to them and their profession a hearty and sincere God Speed.

Frank Benson's tour of *Julius Caesar* in 1893, designed by Alma Tadema

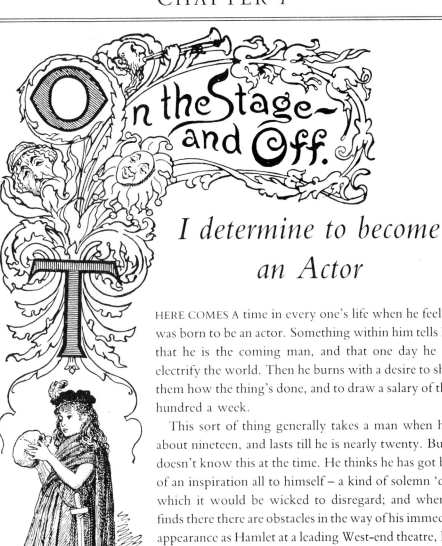

· CHAPTER *1* ·

On the Stage – and Off.

I determine to become an Actor

THERE COMES A time in every one's life when he feels he was born to be an actor. Something within him tells him that he is the coming man, and that one day he will electrify the world. Then he burns with a desire to show them how the thing's done, and to draw a salary of three hundred a week.

This sort of thing generally takes a man when he is about nineteen, and lasts till he is nearly twenty. But he doesn't know this at the time. He thinks he has got hold of an inspiration all to himself – a kind of solemn 'call', which it would be wicked to disregard; and when he finds there there are obstacles in the way of his immediate appearance as Hamlet at a leading West-end theatre, he is blighted.

I myself caught it in the usual course. I was at the theatre one evening seeing *Romeo and Juliet* played, when it suddenly flashed across me that that was my vocation. I thought that all acting was making love in tights to pretty women, and I determined to devote my life to it. When I communicated my heroic resolution to my friends, they reasoned with me. That is, they called me a fool; and then said that they had always thought me a sensible fellow, though that was the first I had ever heard of it.

But I was not to be turned from my purpose.

I commenced operations by studying the great British dramatists. I was practical enough to know that some sort of preparation was necessary, and I thought that, for a beginning, I could not do better than this. Accordingly, I read through every word of Shakspeare, – with notes, which made it still more unintelligible, – Ben Jonson, Beaumont and Fletcher, Sheridan, Goldsmith, and Lord Lytton. This brought me into a state of mind bordering on insanity. Another standard dramatist, and I should have gone raving mad: of that I feel sure. Thinking that a change would do me good, I went in for farces and burlesques, but found them more depressing than the tragedies, and the idea then began to force itself upon me that, taking one consideration with another, an actor's lot would not be a happy one. Just when I was getting most despondent, however, I came across a little book on the art of 'making-up', and this resuscitated me.

'I commenced operations by studying the great British dramatists.'

I suppose the love of 'making-up' is inherent in the human race. I remember belonging, when a boy, to 'The West London United Concert and Entertainment Association'. We used to meet once a week for the purpose of regaling our relations with original songs and concertina solos, and on these occasions we regularly burnt-corked our hands and faces. There was no earthly reason for doing so, and I am even inclined to think we should have made our friends less unhappy if we had spared them this extra attraction. None of our songs had the slightest reference to Dinah. We didn't even ask each other conundrums; while, as for the jokes, they all came from the audience. And yet we daubed ourselves black with as much scrupulousness as if it had been some indispensable religious rite. It could only have been vanity.

'Making-up' certainly assists the actor to a very great degree. At least I found it so in my case. I am naturally of mild and gentle appearance, and, at that time, was particularly so. It was no earthly use my standing in front of the glass and trying to rehearse the part of, say, a drunken costermonger. It was perfectly impossible for me to imagine myself the character. I am ashamed to have to confess it, but I looked more like a young curate than a drunken costermonger, or even a sober one, and the delusion could not be sustained for a moment. It was just the same when I tried to turn myself into a desperate villain; there was nothing of the desperate villain about me. I might, perhaps, have imagined myself going for a walk on Sunday, or saying 'bother it,' or even playing ha'penny nap, but as for ill-treating a lovely and unprotected female, or murdering my grandfather, the thing was absurd. I could not look myself in the face and do it. It was outraging every law of Lavater. My fiercest scowl was a milk- and-watery accompaniment to my blood-thirsty speeches; and when I tried to smile sardonically, I merely looked imbecile.

But crape hair and the rouge pot changed all this. The character of Hamlet stood revealed to me the moment that I put on false eyebrows, and made my cheeks look hollow. With a sallow complexion, dark eyes, and long hair, I *was* Romeo, and, until I washed my face, loved Juliet to the exclusion of all my female cousins. Humour came quite natural when I had a rose nose; and, with a scrubby, black beard, I felt fit for any amount of crime.

My efforts to study elocution, however, were not so successful. I had the misfortune to possess a keen sense of the ludicrous, and to have a morbid dread of appearing

'I . . . loved Juliet to the exclusion of all my female cousins.'

ridiculous. My extreme sensitiveness on this point would have been enough to prevent my ever acting well under any circumstances, and, as it was, it hampered and thwarted me at every turn: not only on the stage, but even in my own room with the door locked. I was always in a state of terror lest any one should overhear me, and half my time was taken up in listening on one side of the keyhole, to make sure that no one was listening on the other; while the slightest creak on the stairs was sufficient to make me stop short in the middle of a passage, and commence whistling or humming in an affectedly careless manner, in order to suggest the idea that I was only amusing myself. I tried getting up early and going to Hampstead Heath, but it was no good. If I could have gone to the Desert of Sahara, and assured myself, by the aid of a powerful telescope, that no living creature was within twenty miles of me, I might have come out strong, but not else. Any confidence I might have placed in Hampstead Heath was rudely dissipated on the very second morning of my visits. Buoyed up by the belief that I was far from every vestige of the madding crowd, I had become quite reckless, and, having just delivered, with great vigour, the oration of Antony over the body of Caesar, I was about starting on something else, when I heard a loud whisper come from some furze bushes close behind me: 'Ain't it proper, Liza! Joe, you run and tell 'Melia to bring Johnny.'

I did not wait for Johnny. I left that spot at the rate of six miles an hour. When I got to Camden Town I looked behind me, cautiously. No crowd appeared to be following me, and I felt relieved, but I did not practise on Hampstead Heath again.

After about two months of this kind of thing, I was satisfied that I had learned all that could possibly be required, and that I was ready to 'come out'. But here the question

An audition, 1889

very naturally arose, 'How can I get out?' My first idea was to write to one of the leading managers, tell him frankly my ambition, and state my abilities in a modest but straightforward manner. To this, I argued, he would reply by requesting me to call upon him, and let him see for himself what I could do. I should then go to the theatre at the time appointed, and send up my card. He would ask me into his private room, and, after a little general conversation on the weather, and the latest murder, etc., etc., he would suggest my rehearsing some short scene before him, or reciting one or two speeches. This I should do in a way that would quite astonish him, and he would engage me on the spot at a small salary. I did not expect much at first, but fancied that five or six pounds per week would be near the mark. After that, the rest would be easy. I should go on for some months, perhaps a year, without making any marked sensation. Then my opportunity would come. A new play would be produced, in which there would be some minor part, not considered of any importance, but which in my hands (I had just read the history of 'Lord Dundreary', and believed every word of it) would become the great thing in the play, and the talk of London.

I should take the town by storm, make the fortune of my manager, and be the leading actor of the day. I used to dwell on the picture of the night when I should first startle the world. I could see the vast house before me with its waves of wild, excited faces. I could hear their hoarse roar of applause ringing in my ears. Again and again I bowed before them, and again and again the cheers burst forth, and my name was shouted with waving of hats and with bravos.

I did not write to a manager, though, after all. A friend who knew something about the subject said he wouldn't if he were me, and I didn't.

I asked him what course he would advise, and he said: 'Go to an agent, and tell him just exactly what you want.' I went to two or three agents, and told them all just exactly what I wanted, and they were equally frank, and told me just exactly what *they* wanted, which, speaking generally, was five shillings booking fee, to begin with. To do them justice, though, I must say that none of them appeared at all anxious to have me; neither did they hold out to me much hope of making my fortune. I believe my name is still down in the books of most of the agents – at least, I have never been round to take it off – and I expect that amongst them they will obtain for me a first-class engagement one of these days, when I am Bishop of London, or editor of a society paper, or something of that sort.

It was not for want of worrying that they did not do anything for me then. I was for

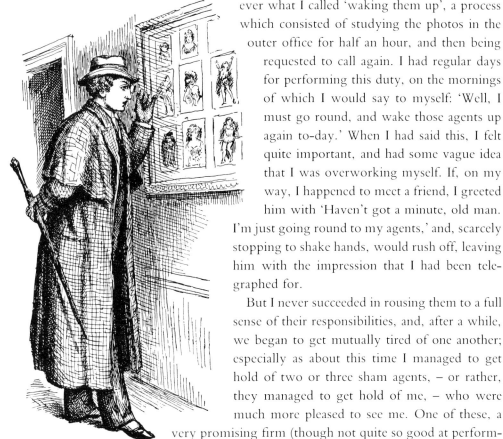

ever what I called 'waking them up', a process which consisted of studying the photos in the outer office for half an hour, and then being requested to call again. I had regular days for performing this duty, on the mornings of which I would say to myself: 'Well, I must go round, and wake those agents up again to-day.' When I had said this, I felt quite important, and had some vague idea that I was overworking myself. If, on my way, I happened to meet a friend, I greeted him with 'Haven't got a minute, old man. I'm just going round to my agents,' and, scarcely stopping to shake hands, would rush off, leaving him with the impression that I had been tele- graphed for.

But I never succeeded in rousing them to a full sense of their responsibilities, and, after a while, we began to get mutually tired of one another; especially as about this time I managed to get hold of two or three sham agents, – or rather, they managed to get hold of me, – who were much more pleased to see me. One of these, a very promising firm (though not quite so good at perform- ing), had its offices then in Leicester Square, and consisted of two partners, one of whom, however, was always in the country on important business, and could never be seen. I remember they got four pounds out of me, for which they undertook, in writing, to obtain me a salaried London engagement before the expiration of a month. Just when the time was nearly up, however, I received a long and sympathetic letter from the mysterious travelling partner. This hitherto rusticating individual had, it appeared, returned to town the previous day, but only to discover a state of things that had shocked him beyond all expression. His partner, the one to whom I had paid the four pounds, besides defrauding nearly all the clients by taking money for engagements which he had no possible means of obtaining, had robbed him, the writer of the letter,

Set direction for *Robert and the Devil*, Prince's Theatre, Bristol

of upwards of seventy pounds, and had bolted, no one knew whither. My present correspondent expressed himself deeply grieved at my having been so villainously cheated, and hoped I would join him in taking proceedings against his absconding partner – when found. He concluded by stating that four pounds was an absurd sum to charge for obtaining such an engagement as had been held out to me, and that if I would give him (who really had the means of performing his promises) two pounds, he would get me one in a week, or ten days at the outside. Would I call and see him that evening? I did not go that evening, but I went the first thing the next morning. I then found the door locked, and a notice on it that all letters were to be left with the housekeeper. Coming down stairs, I met a man coming up, and asked him if he knew where either of the partners could be found. He said that he would give a sovereign to know, and that he was the landlord. I heard of the firm again the other day, and I believe it is still flourishing, though with the customary monthly change as to name and address. By the bye, I wonder if the agent nuisance will ever be stamped out. Perhaps, now that education is compulsory, the next generation of actors and managers may be able to look after their own affairs, and so dispense with the interference of these meddlers on commission.

CHAPTER 2

I become an Actor

MONG THE SHAM agents must be classed the 'Professors', or 'X.Y.Z.s', who are always 'able to place two or three' (never more than two or three: it would be no use four applying) 'lady and gentlemen amateurs, of tall or medium stature, either dark or fair, but *must* be of good appearance, at a leading West-end theatre, in good parts: Salaried engagement.' These gentlemen are appreciative, and very quick to discern real talent. They perceived mine in a moment. They were all of them sure that I should make a splendid actor, and I was just the man they wanted. But they were conscientious. They scorned to hide the truth, and told me of my faults without reserve. They said that I was full of promise, that I had the makings of a really great actor in me, *but* – and the remarkable part of it was that no two of them agreed as to that 'but'. One said it was my voice. All that I wanted was to train my voice; then I should be perfect. Another thought my voice was a very fine one, but told me that my attitudes would not do at all. When my attitudes were a little more artistic, he could get me an engagement at once. A third, after hearing me recite a trifle or two from *Macbeth*, clapped me on the shoulder, and insisted on shaking hands. There were tears almost in his eyes, and he appeared quite overcome. He said:

'My boy, you have got it in you. You are an actor! but – you want chic.'

I had not got the slightest notion what he meant. I said: 'You think so.'

He was sure of it. It would be impossible for me to succeed without chic: *with* chic, I should soon be famous. I determined, at any price, to get chic, and I deferentially put it to him how he thought I could obtain it. He paused for a minute or so, evidently considering how it could be done, while I stood anxiously awaiting the result. Suddenly a bright idea seemed to strike him. He laid his hand confidentially on my arm, and in the impressive voice of a man who is communicating some extraordinary discovery, said:

'Come to me, twice a week, Tuesdays and Fridays, say from eight to nine.' Then he drew back a few paces to see what effect it had upon me.

I replied that I supposed he meant he would teach it me. He seemed struck with my intelligence, and acknowledged that that was just precisely what he did mean. He explained – always in the same strictly confidential manner, as though he would not for the world have any one else know – that he had had great experience in this particular branch of dramatic education. He had letters now in his desk from well-known actors and actresses, persons of the greatest eminence, acknowledging that they owed their present position entirely to his teaching, and thanking him for all that he had done for them. He would shew me those letters, and he rose to do so. But no, on second thoughts he would not; they were written in confidence, and it would not be right for him to let others see them – not even me, whom he felt he could trust. To do him justice, he never did shew those letters, either to me, or, as far as I could learn, to any one else, though I subsequently came across three or four people who expressed an earnest desire to see them.

But I was slowly and painfully gaining experience, and I went away without leaving the five-pound note, which I – 'as a man of business' – ought to have seen was an absurdly small amount, his usual charge being twenty guineas; only, somehow or other, he had taken an interest in me, and felt sure I should reflect credit on his teaching, and so make it up to him in that way.

Another class that make a very good thing out of stage-struck asses, are the 'managers' (?) who have vacancies for 'an amateur lady and gentleman in a specially selected company'. They are men who evidently believe in the literal truth of Jacques's opinion as to all men and women being players, for they put raw novices into the leading parts with a confidence as to the result that is simply touching. The Thespian aspirant, who has never acted out of his own back parlour, feels a little nervous,

Outside the theatre, 1850

though, at being cast for Banquo and Colonel Damas, to open with on the following Saturday. He cannot quite make up his mind, whether a mistake has been made, a practical joke played upon him for the amusement of the rest of the company, or whether it is that the manager is really an intelligent man, who knows ability when he sees it. He does not like to speak about it, lest it should be thought he was not confident of his own powers – a failing of which the stage tyro is not usually guilty. Besides which, the parts might be taken from him, and this he by no means desires, although, at the same time, he is perfectly sure that he could play every other character in the piece much better. I had only one experience of the sham manager – at least of this kind of sham manager. Unfortunately there are other kinds, as most actors know to their cost, but these I have not come to yet. No, and I wish I had never gone to them, either.

There were about half a dozen of us noodles who had answered one advertisement, and we met every night for rehearsals at a certain house in Newman Street. Three or four well-known professionals, who were then starring in the province, but who would join us at the beginning of the next week, were to fill the chief parts, and we were to start for Gravesend immediately after their arrival. I had been engaged at a weekly salary of one pound fifteen shillings, and had been cast for the parts of Gilbert Featherstone in *Lost in London*, and the King in *Hamlet*. Everything went smoothly; there had been no suggestion of a premium or anything of that kind; and, although I had, by this time, grown exceedingly suspicious, I began to think that this, at all events, was not a swindle. But I soon found out the trick. On the fifth night of the rehearsals, our manager was particularly pleasant, and complimented me on what he called my really original reading of the parts. During the pauses he leant familiarly on my shoulder, and discussed the piece with me. We had a little argument about the part of the King. He differed from me, at first, on one or two points, but afterwards came round to my views, and admitted that I was right. Then he asked me how I was going to dress the part. I had thought of this,

even before I had studied the words, so I was as pat as could be on
the subject, and we went through all the details, and arranged
for a very gorgeous costume, indeed. He did
not try to stint me in the least, though I was
once or twice afraid he might grumble at the
cost. But no, he seemed quite as anxious as I
was that the thing should be done in good
style. It would be a little expensive, as he
himself said, but then, 'you may just as well
do the thing properly, while you are about
it,' he added, and I agreed with him. He
went on to reckon up the amount. He
said that he could get the things very
cheap – much cheaper than any one else, as
he had a friend in the business, who would
let him have them for exactly what they
cost to make. I congratulated him on the
fact, but, feeling no personal interest in the
matter, began to be rather bored by his
impressiveness on the subject. After
adding it all up, he came to the conclusion
that nine pounds ought to cover the lot.

'And very cheap, too,' said he; 'the things will be good, and will always come in
useful'; and I agreed with him again, and remarked that I thought they would be well
worth the money; but wondered what on earth all this had got to do with me.

Then he wanted to know whether I would pay the money that evening, or bring it
with me next time.

'Me! me pay!' I exclaimed, rendered ungrammatical by surprise. 'What for?'

'What for! Why, for the costume,' replied he; 'you can't play the part without, and if
you got the things yourself, you'd have to pay about four pounds more, that's all. If
you haven't got all the money handy,' he continued soothingly, 'let me have as much
as you can, you know, and I'll try and get my friend to trust you for the rest.'

On subsequent inquiry among the others, I found that three of them had already let
him have about five pounds each, and that a fourth intended to hand him over four

pounds ten the following night. I and another agreed to wait and see. We did not see much, however. We never saw the well-known professionals, and, after the next evening, we never saw our manager again. Those who had paid saw less.

I now thought I would try hunting for myself, without the aid of agents or advertisements. I might be more successful, and certainly could not be less. The same friend that had recommended me not to write to the managers, concurred with me in this view, and thought I could not do better than drop in occasionally at 'The Occidental'; and I accordingly so dropped in. I suppose there is no actor who does not know 'The Occidental', though it does try to hide itself down a dark court, being, no doubt, of a retiring disposition, like the rest of the profession.

I found the company there genial and pleasant, and without any objection to drinking at my expense. When, however, I hinted my wish to join the profession, they regarded me with a look of the most profound pity, and seemed really quite concerned. They shook their heads gravely, told me their own experiences, and did all they could to dissuade me from my intention. But I looked upon them as selfish fellows who wanted to keep young talent from the stage. Even if their advice was given honestly, I argued, it was no use taking any notice of it. Every one thinks his own calling the worst, and if a man waited to enter a profession until those already in it recommended him to, he might sit and twiddle his thumbs for the rest of his life. So I paid no attention to their warning, but continued in my course, and, at length, found some one to help me.

He was a large, flabby-looking individual, who seemed to live on Scotch whisky and big cigars, and was never either drunk or sober. He did not smell refreshing – a fact he made all the more impressive by breathing very hard, right into one's face, while talking. He had formerly been a country manager, but how he earned his livelihood now, was always a mystery to me, as, although he rented a dirty little back room in a street leading out of the Strand, and called it his office, he never did anything there but go to sleep. He was, however, well known to the theatrical frequenters of 'The Occidental', – better known than respected, as I afterwards learnt, – while he himself knew everybody, and it appeared to me that he was just the very man I wanted. At first, he was not any more enthusiastic than the others, but my mentioning that I was prepared to pay a small premium in order to obtain an appearance, set him pondering, and, in the end, he didn't see why it could not be done. When I stated the figure I was ready to give, he grew more hopeful still, and came to the conclusion that it *could* be

The pantomime at the Princess's Theatre, London, January 1864

done. He did not even see why I should not make a big name, if I only left myself entirely in his hands.

'I have done the same thing for other people,' said he, 'and I can for you, if I like. There is ——,' he went on, getting talkative all at once, 'he is drawing his eighty pounds a week now. Well, damn it all, sir, I made that man – made him. He'd never have been anything more than a third-rate provincial actor, if it hadn't been for me. Then look at ——, at the ——, I knew him when he was having twenty-two shillings a week for responsibles, with old Joe Clamp, and that only when he could get it, mind you. I brought him up to London, started him at the Surrey, took him on to the West-end, and worked him up to what he is. And now, when he passed me in his brougham, he don't know me,' and my new-found friend heaved a sigh, and took another pull to drown his grief at the ingratitude of human nature.

'Yes, sir,' he continued, on emerging from his glass, 'I made those men and why shouldn't I make you?'

As I could not shew any reason for his not doing so, he determined that he would; although he supposed that I should turn out just the same as the rest of them, and forget him, when I was at the top of the tree. But I assured him most solemnly that I would not, and that I should be just as pleased to see him, when I was a great man, as I was then, and I shook hands warmly with him, as a token of how pleased I was to see him then; for I felt really grateful to him for the favours he was going to bestow on me, and I was quite vexed that he should think I might prove ungrateful, and neglect him.

When I saw him the next day, he told me he had done it. He had arranged an engagement for me with a Surrey-side manager, to whom he would introduce me to-morrow, when the agreement could be signed, and everything settled. I was, accordingly, to be at his office for the purpose at eleven o'clock the following morning – and to bring the money with me. That was his parting injunction.

I did not walk back to my lodgings, I skipped back. I burst open the door, and went up the stairs like a whirlwind; but I was too excited to stop indoors. I went and had dinner at a first-class restaurant, the bill for which considerably lessened my slender means. 'Never mind,' I thought, 'what are a few shillings, when I shall soon be earning my hundreds of pounds.' I went to the theatre, but I don't know what theatre it was, or what was the play, and I don't think I knew at the time. I did notice the acting a little, but only to fancy how much better I could play each part myself. I wondered how I should like these particular actors and actresses, when I came to know them. I thought I should rather like the leading lady, and, in my imagination, sketched out the details of a most desperate flirtation with her, that would send all the other actors mad with jealousy. Then I went home to bed, and lay awake all night dreaming.

I got up at seven the next morning, and hurried over my breakfast, so as to be in time for the appointment at eleven. I think I looked at my watch (I wonder where that watch is, now!) at least every other minute. I got down to the Strand a little before ten, and wandered up and down a small portion of it, frightened to go a stone's throw from the office, and yet dreading to go too near it. I bought a new pair of gloves. I remember they were salmon colour, and one of them split as I was trying to get it on, so I carried it crumpled up in my hand, and wore the other one. When it got within twenty minutes of the time, I turned into the street where the office was, and loitered about there, with an uncomfortable feeling that every one living in it knew what I had come

about, and was covertly watching me from behind blinds and curtains. It seemed as though eleven o'clock never would come, but Big Ben tolled it out at last, and I walked to the door, trying to look as if I had just strolled up.

When I reached the office, no one was there, and the door was locked. My heart sank within me. Had the whole thing been a cruel hoax? Was it to be another disappointment? Had the manager been murdered? Had the theatre been burned down? Why were they not here? Something extraordinary must have happened to make them late on such an important occasion as this. I spent half an hour of intense suspense, and then they arrived. They hoped they had not kept me waiting, and I replied, 'Oh no, not at all,' and murmured something about having only just come myself.

As soon as we all three were inside the little office, I was introduced to the manager, who turned out to be an actor I had often seen on the boards, but who did not look a bit like himself, though he would have done very well for his own son; he was so much shorter and younger than he ought to have been. The clean-shaven face gives actors such a youthful appearance. It was difficult to believe, at first, that the sedate-looking boys I used to meet at rehearsal, were middle-aged men with families, some of them.

Altogether, my future manager did not realize my expectations of him. He was not dressed with that reckless disregard for expense, that I had looked for in a man of his position. To tell the truth, he presented a very seedy figure indeed. I put it down, however, to that contempt for outward appearance, so often manifested by men of great wealth, and called to mind stories of millionaires who had gone about almost in rags; and I remembered, too, how I had once seen the mother of one of our leading burlesque actresses, and how I had been surprised at her extreme dinginess – the mother's.

They had the agreements all ready, and the manager and I signed in each other's presence, and exchanged. Then I handed him a ten-pound note, and he gave me a receipt for it. Everything was strictly formal. The agreement, especially, was very plain and precise, and there could be no mistake about it. It arranged for me to give my services for the first month gratis, and after that I was to receive a *salary according to ability*. This seemed to me very fair, indeed. If anything, it was, perhaps, a little reckless on his part, and might press heavily upon him. He told me candidly, however, that he did not think I should be worth more than thirty shillings a week to him for the first two or three months, though, of course, it would depend upon myself entirely, and he should be only too pleased if it proved otherwise. I held a different opinion on the subject, but did not mention it, thinking it would be better to wait and let time prove it. So I merely said I wished for nothing but what was fair and just, and it appearing that this was exactly what he wanted me to have, we parted on the best of terms: but not before all particulars had been arranged. He was going to open for the summer season in three weeks' time, and the rehearsals were to commence about a fortnight before. For the next week, therefore, I was nothing; after that, I was an Actor!!!★

★ My friends deny this. They say I never became an actor. I say I did, and I think I ought to know.

The gymnast in a music hall production, 1893

· CHAPTER 3 ·

Through the Stage Door

I T WAS NOT until about a week before the opening night, that I received a summons to attend at the theatre. Eleven o'clock was the time appointed for 'the company to assemble on the stage', and, accordingly, at a few minutes before that hour, I stood in front of the stage door.

It was a dingy-looking place, up a back street, with a barber's shop on one side, and a coal shed on the other. A glorious spring sunshine made it look, by contrast, still more uninviting, and I likened it to the entrance to the enchanted palace in the fairy tales, where the gloomier the portal through which the prince passes, the more gorgeous the halls beyond. This was before I had seen the inside.

But it wouldn't do for me to stop there meditating. It was already two minutes past eleven, and the rest of the company would be waiting for me. I laid my hand upon the latch, and ——

A moment, please. Before I throw open that door and let daylight in upon the little world beyond, let me offer a word or two of preparatory explanation.

The theatrical world is a big world. From one of the leading London theatres to a travelling booth (I intend no slighting allusion to our talented American cousins) is a wide stretch, and embraces a great variety. My experience was confined to three or four of these varieties, and by no means extended to the whole. My short career was passed among the minor London theatres and second and third rate travelling companies; and it is of these, and these only,

'I stood in front of the stage door.'

that I shall speak. But of these – of what came under my actual observation, that is – I shall speak freely, endeavouring to record things exactly as I found them – nothing extenuating, nor setting down aught in malice. It may be that, in the course of my comments, I shall think it necessary to make a few more or less sensible and original remarks; to tell actors and actresses what they ought to do, and what they ought not to do; to explain to managers how they ought to manage their own business; and to give good advice generally all round. Therefore, at the outset, I wish it to be clearly understood that, when so doing, I have in mind only that part of the theatrical world with which I am acquainted. As regards such theatres as, for example, the Lyceum or the St James's, they are managed quite as well, perhaps, as I could manage them myself, and I have no fault to find with them. Even if I had, I should not do so here, for in these reminiscences I intend to talk only about what I understand – an eccentric resolution for an author, I admit; but no matter, I like to be original, now and then. With this understanding we will push back the door and enter.

I found a wheezy little old man inside, boxed up behind a glass partition, toasting a bloater before a small fire. On that morning I felt kindly disposed towards all living things, and I therefore spoke kindly, even to this poor old buffer. I said:

'Good morning. It's a fine day.'

He said, 'Shut the door, can't yer; or else get outside.'

Acting on this suggestion, I shut the door, and then stood leaning against it, while he finished toasting the bloater. When I saw that this operation was completed, I had another try at him. I remarked that my name was ——. Of course, I had assumed a stage name. They all do it. Heaven only knows why; I am sure *they* don't. While in the profession, I met a young fellow whose real name happened to be the very one that I had assumed, while he had taken my real name for his assumed one. We were both happy and contented enough, until we met; but afterwards, we took a sadder view of life, with all its shams and vanities.

As the mere announcement of my name had no visible effect on the stage-door keeper – for such I found him to be – I fired my last shot, and told him I was an actor. It roused him. It electrified him to such a degree, that he took his gaze off the bloater, and looked at me. Having feasted his eyes upon me to his full satisfaction, he said, 'Down the yard,' and returned to what, I suppose, was his breakfast; there being a dismal, just-got-up sort of look about him.

Gathering from this, that there was a yard somewhere in the neighbourhood, and that, when I had found it, I was to go down it, I started off to look for it. I discovered it at last, quite unexpectedly, by the process of stumbling over a friendly cat, and bursting open a door with my head. The moment I got into it, I was surrounded by at least half a dozen of the feline species. They looked hungry, and welcomed me with enthusiasm, under an absurd idea that I was the cat's-meat man, whom I did not resemble in the least. Cats are kept at theatres to keep away the rats, but sometimes the cats themselves become so numerous, as to be rather more of a nuisance than the rats, and then it is necessary to keep some one to keep away the cats. They take a great interest in the drama, these cats. They always make a point of coming on in the middle of the most pathetic scenes, when they take the centre of the stage, and proceed to go through one or other of their decidedly peculiar toilet exercises.

Going down the yard, as directed, and groping my way through a dark passage at the end, I found myself in a vast, gloomy vault, full of hollow echoes, and strange, shapeless shadows; at least, that is what it seemed to me.

I cannot say, now, what notions I had previously formed of 'behind the scenes.' They were dispelled so rudely and suddenly, that all trace of them is lost. I know they were formed; partly by Dower Wilson's charming sketches, where fairy damsels (in the costume of their country) lean gracefully against the back of the landscapes, with their pretty legs crossed; partly by the descriptions of friends who said they had been there; and partly from my own imagination – a vivid one. The reality, however, exceeded my wildest expectations. I could never have dreamt of anything so utterly dismal as an empty theatre by daylight, or rather day-darkness. No, not even after a supper of beefsteaks and porter.

At first, I could see nothing; but, after a while, I got used to the dimness, and was

A scene painter backstage at the Theatre Royal, Birmingham, *c.* 1901

able to look about me. The decorations of the place (such as they were – such as might be expected in a theatre where the stalls were three shillings, and the gallery fourpence) were shrouded in dirty white cloths. The music stools and stands in the orchestra, together with the big drum, and the violoncello in a green baize case, were all in a heap in the corner, as if they had had a performance on their own account during the night, and had ended up by getting drunk. This idea was further suggested by the appearance of the gallery bar, which could be seen from the stage, though it looked about half a mile off, and which was crowded with empty bottles and dirty pewter pots and glasses. Shabby, patched scenery – a mere unintelligible daub, seen close to – was littered all round me; propped up against the great wooden beams which supported the flies, or against the side walls; piled up at the back, in what was called the 'scene dock;' lying down flat at my feet; or hanging suspended over my head. In the centre of the stage was a rickety table, and on the table was a candle, stuck in a ginger-beer bottle. A solitary sunbeam, having sneaked in through some odd crevice, threw a band of light across the gloom, and showed up the dust, of which the place seemed full. A woman, with a noisy cold in her head, was sweeping out the pit; and some unseen animal, which I

judged to be a small boy, by the noise it made, was performing a shrill whistle somewhere in the region of the dress circle. The roar from the street sounded dull and muffled, but the banging of a door, or the falling of a chair within the building, made such a noise, that the spiders ran into their holes for fright.

CHAPTER 4

Behind the Scenes

I HAD THE stage all to myself for about half an hour. It is the etiquette of the theatre for every one to be late. You estimate the position of an actor, by the time he is late for rehearsal. If he (I don't say a word about ladies: they are always an hour late for everything, bless 'em) is twenty minutes behind, he is most likely mere utility. If a man keeps everybody waiting an hour and a half, you may put him down as a star.

I occupied the time pleasantly enough in wandering about, and finding out all I could. I climbed up a shaky wooden staircase to the 'flies', and looked down upon the stage from a height of fifty feet. I scrambled about up there amidst ladders, and small platforms, and ropes, and pulleys, and wind-lasses, and gas pipes, and empty gas bags, and beer cans, and darkness, and dust. Then, up another ladder, leading higher still, and along a narrow plank, crossing from one side of the stage to the other, over a perfect hanging forest of scenery.

Clambering round behind, I came to the scene-painting room. It was a long, narrow sort of loft, forty feet above the stage. One side of it was of canvas – part of an enormous sheet, which passed right through it, in at the top and out at the bottom. This sheet of canvas, on which a scene was being painted, was suspended from the roof of the theatre by means of pulleys, so that the whole could be raised or lowered at pleasure, and every portion of it brought within reach of the scene-painter, without his moving.

If I have not explained myself clearly, try this: Take your wife's best travelling trunk (choosing a time when she is not at home), wrench the cover off, and then hold the box up against the window blind, in such a position that the blind is where the cover would have been. There you have it. The box is the scene-painter's room – the blind, the scene.

There was plenty of light and colour (the latter in buckets) in the room, but very little else. A long, deal table, crowded with brushes and paint pots, ran nearly the whole length of it. The scene-painter's palette, a marble slab about six feet square, lay on the floor, and, near it, one of the brushes with which the sky had been laid on. This brush was the size of an ordinary carpet broom. Noting these things, I left the studio, and descended.

A little lower down was the wardrobe room. There was not much in it though. Dresses are borrowed as they are wanted, now, from the costumiers round Covent Garden and Drury Lane; everything being found for so much a week. Years ago, I believe, each theatre used to make, and keep, its own costumes. Even now, a few old-fashioned provincial houses have a substantial wardrobe attached to them, but these are the exceptions, and, as a rule, little, if anything, is kept in stock. Here, there were a few pairs of very loose and baggy-looking tights, half a dozen rusty tin helmets, a heap of buff shoes in a corner – half of them right, half left, sort 'em as you want 'em – some natty waistcoats – red and blue, with a dash of yellow; the sort of thing stage Yorkshiremen wear when they come to London, black cloaks for any one who might wish to dissemble, and an assortment of spangled things. These were the principal items, all of which had seen their best days.

Between the yard and the stage was a very big room, containing so heterogeneous a collection of articles that, at first, I fancied it must be a co-operative store in connection with the theatre. It was, however, only the property room, the things therein being properties, or, more commonly 'props', so called, I believe, because they help to

support the drama. I will give you some of the contents of
the room haphazard as I recollect them. There was a
goodly number of tin cups, painted black up to within half
an inch of the rim, so as to give them the appearance of
being always full. It is from these vessels that the
happy peasantry carouses, and the comic army gets
helplessly fuddled. There is a universality about
them. They are of the one touch of (stage)
nature which makes the whole world kin.
They are used alike by the Esquimaux
and the Hottentot. The Roman
soldiery appear never to have drunk
out of anything else; while, without them, the French Revolution
would lose its chief characteristic.
Besides these common cups, there were gold
and silver ones, used only for banquets, and
high-class suicides. There were bottles, and glasses,
and jugs, and decanters. From these aids to debauchery, it
was pleasant to turn to a cozy-looking tea service on a tray with a white table cloth;
there was a soothing suggestion of muffins and domestic bliss about it. There was
plenty of furniture, a couple of tables, a bedstead, a dresser, a sofa, chairs – half a dozen
of them, high-backed ones, for 'hall in the old Grange', etc.: they were made by fixing
pasteboard backs on to ordinary cane chairs. The result was that they were top heavy,
and went over at the slightest touch; so that picking them up, and trying to make them
stand, formed the chief business of the scenes in which they were used.

I remember the first time our light comedy attempted to sit down on one of these
chairs. It was on the opening night. He had just said something funny, and, having said
it, sat down, crossed his legs, and threw himself back, with all that easy, negligent
grace so peculiarly his own. Legs were the only things that could be seen for the next
few minutes.

Other 'props' were, a throne, gorgeous in gilt paper and glazed calico; a fire-grate,
stuffed with red tinfoil; a mirror, made with silver paper; a bunch of jailer's keys;
handcuffs; leg irons; flat irons; rifles; brooms; bayonets; picks and crowbars for the

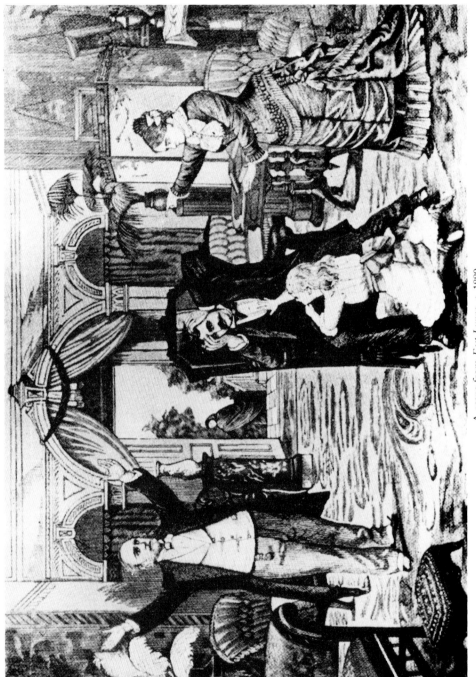

A scene from *East Lynne*, c. 1889

virtuously infuriated populace; clay pipes; daggers made of wood; stage broadswords – there is no need to describe these, everybody knows them; they are like nothing else on earth – battle axes; candlesticks; a pound or two of short dips; a crown, set with diamonds and rubies each as big as a duck's egg; a cradle – empty, an affecting sight; carpets, kettles, and pots; a stretcher; a chariot; a bunch of carrots; a costermonger's barrow; banners; a leg of mutton, and a baby. Everything, in short, that could possibly be wanted, either in a palace or a garret, a farmyard or a battlefield.

Still wandering about, I came across a hole in the floor at the side of the stage, and groped my way down a ladder to the region beneath, where the fairies come from, and the demons go to. It was perfectly dark, and I could see nothing. It smelt very mouldy, and seemed to be full of cunning contrivances for barking your shins. After bumping myself about a good deal there, I was glad to find my way out again, deferring all further investigations to some future period, with a candle.

On emerging, I saw that the company had at last began to arrive. A tall, solemn-looking man was pacing the stage, and him I greeted. He was the stage manager, and so of course rather surly. I don't know why stage managers are always surly, but they are.

In the course of the next few minutes, there trotted in a demure-looking little man, who turned out to be our 'first low comedy', and very good low comedy he was, too, though, from his wooden expression, you might have thought him as destitute of humour, as the librettist of a comic opera. Then followed the heavy man, talking in a very gruff voice to a good-looking young fellow with him, who played the juveniles when our manager didn't take them himself. Then after a short interval, a lady – an old queer-looking little lady, who walked with a stick, and complained of rheumatism, and, who, as soon as she reached the stage, plumped herself down on the thick end of a mossy bank, from which nothing would induce her to rise until she got up to go home. She was our 'old woman'. She did the doting mothers and the comic old maids. She had played everything in her time, and could play anything still. She would have taken Juliet or Juliet's nurse, whichever you liked, and have done both of them well. She would have been ten minutes making up for Juliet, and then, sitting in the middle of the pit, you would have put her down for twenty.

The next to appear was a gentleman ('walking') in a fur trimmed overcoat, patent-leather boots and white gaiters and lavender kid gloves. He carried a silver-headed cane in his hand, a glass in his left eye, a cigar in his mouth (put out as soon as he got to the stage, of course), and a small nosegay in his button hole. His salary I subsequently discovered to be thirty shillings a week. After him, came two ladies (not with any designs upon the young man: merely in the order of time). One of them was thin and pale, with a careworn look underneath the rouge, just as if she was some poor, hard-worked woman, with a large family and small means, instead of an actress. The other was fair, fat, and – forty, if she was a day. She was gorgeously 'got up', both as regards complexion and dress. I can't describe the latter, because I never can tell what any woman has got on. I only know she conveyed an impression to my mind of being stuck out all round, and thrown out in front, and puffed out at the back, and towering up at the top, and trailing away behind, and all to such a degree, that she looked four times her natural size. As everybody was very glad indeed to see her, and welcomed her with what seemed to be irrepressible joy, even the stage manager being civil, I naturally concluded that she was the embodiment of all the virtues known to human kind. The whispered remarks that I overheard, however, did not quite support this view, and I was at a loss to reconcile matters, until I learned that she was the manager's wife. She was the leading lady, and the characters she particularly affected, and in which she was affected, were the girlish heroines, and the children who die young and go to heaven.

The rest of the company was made up of a couple of very old men, and a middle-aged stout one, two rather pretty girls, evidently possessed of an inexhaustible fund of humour, for they kept each other giggling all the morning; and the manager himself, who arrived last, and was less interested in the proceedings than any one else. No one took the slightest notice of me, though I purposely stood about in conspicuous positions, and I felt like the new boy at school.

When everybody had arrived, the rickety table was brought down to the front, and a bell rung; whereupon a small boy suddenly appeared for the first time, and was given the 'parts' to distribute. It was a manuscript play, though well known to the company, nearly all of whom had played in it plenty of times before. All the parts were torn and greasy, except one, which was prominently clean. When the boy came to that one, he seemed puzzled, not knowing to whom it belonged; so he stood in the centre of the stage, and bawled out the name on it; and as it was my name, and I had to claim the part, I was at once lifted out of my obscurity, and placed in an opposite extreme hardly more comfortable.

CHAPTER 5

A Rehearsal

I HURRIEDLY UNFOLDED the paper, to see what kind of a part I had got. I was anxious to begin studying it immediately. I had to form my conception of the character, learn the words and business, and get up gesture and expression, all in one week. No time was therefore to be lost. I give the part in extenso:

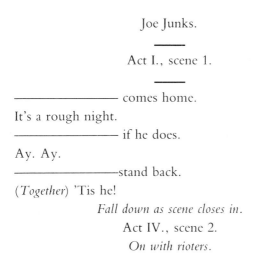

Joe Junks.

———

Act I., scene 1.

———

——————————— comes home.
It's a rough night.
——————————— if he does.
Ay. Ay.
———————————stand back.
(*Together*) 'Tis he!
Fall down as scene closes in.
Act IV., scene 2.
On with rioters.

I was of a sanguine disposition at that time, but I didn't exactly see how I was going to make much of a sensation with *that*. It seemed to me that my talents were being thrown away. An ordinary actor would have done for a part like that. However, if they chose to waste me, it was more their misfortune than mine. I would say nothing, but do the best I could with the thing, and throw as much feeling into the character as it would hold. In truth, I ought to have been very proud of the part, for I found out later on that it had been written specially for me by the manager. Our low comedy, who knew the whole piece by heart, told me this. Then he added musingly, 'A very good idea, too, of the boss's. I always said the first act wanted strengthening.'

At last, everybody having been supplied with his or her part, and the leader of the band having arrived, the rehearsal really commenced. The play was one of the regular old-fashioned melodramas, and the orchestra had all its work cut out to keep up with it. Nearly all the performers had a bar of music to bring them on each time, and another to take them off; a bar when they sat down, and a bar when they got up again; while it took a small overture to get them across the stage. As for the leading lady, every mortal thing she did or said, from remarking that the snow was cold, in the first act, to fancying she saw her mother and then dying, in the last, was preceded by a regular concert. I firmly believe that if, while on the stage, she had shown signs of wanting to sneeze, the band would at once have struck up quick music. I began to think, after a while, that it must be an opera, and to be afraid that I should have to sing my part.

The first scene was between the old landlord of an old inn, some village gossips, and the villain of the piece. The stage manager (who played the villain – naturally) stood in the centre of the stage, from which the rest of the company had retired, and, from there, with the manuscript in his hand, he directed the proceedings.

'Now then, gentlemen,' cried he, 'first scene, please. Hallett, landlord, Bilikins, and Junks' (I was Junks), 'up stage, right. I shall be here' (walking across and stamping his foot on the spot intended), 'sitting at table. All discovered at rise of curtain. You' (turning and speaking to me, about whom he had evidently been instructed), 'you, Mr L., will be sitting at the end, smoking a pipe. Take up your cues sharply, and mind you speak up, or nobody will hear you: this is a big house. What are you going to give us for an overture, Mr P.?' (I call the leader of the band Mr P.) 'Can you give us something old English, just before we ring up? Thanks, do – has a good effect. Now then, please, we will begin, Very piano all through this scene, Mr P., until near the end. I'll tell you where, when we come to it.'

Then, reading from our parts, we commenced. The speeches, with the exception of the very short ones, were not given at full length. The last two or three words, forming the cues, were clearly spoken, but the rest was, as a rule, mumbled through, skipped altogether, or else represented by a droning 'er, er, er,' interspersed with occasional disjointed phrases. A scene of any length, between only two or three of the characters, – and there are many such, – was cut out entirely, and gone through apart

by the people concerned. Thus, while the main rehearsal was proceeding in the centre of the stage, a minor one was generally going on at the same time in some quiet corner – two men fighting a duel with walking sticks; a father denouncing his son, and turning him out of doors; or some dashing young gallant, in a big check ulster, making love to some sweet young damsel, whose little boy, aged seven, was sitting on her lap.

I waited eagerly for my cue, not knowing when it was coming, and, in my anxiety, made two or three false starts. I was put out of any doubt about it, when the time really did come, by a friendly nod from the gentleman who represented the landlord, and thereupon I made my observation as to the dreadful state of the weather in a loud, clear, and distinct voice, as it seemed to me. As, however, nobody appeared to have heard me, and as they were evidently waiting for me, I repeated the information in a louder, clearer, and more distinct voice, if possible; after which the stage manager spoke and said:

'Now then, Mr L., come along, let's have it.'

I explained to him that he had already had it, and he then replied, 'Oh, that will never do at all. You must speak up more than that. Why, even *we* couldn't hear you on the

The theatre at Street, Somerset, c. 1899

stage. Bawl it out. Remember this is a large place; you're not playing in a back drawing-room now.'

I thought it was impossible for me to speak louder than I had without doing myself some serious injury, and I began to pity the gallery boys. Any one never having attempted to speak in a large public building would hardly imagine how weak and insignificant the ordinary conversational tones are, even at their loudest. To make your voice 'carry,' you have to *throw* it out, instead of letting it crawl out when you open your mouth. The art is easily acquired, and, by it, you are able to make your very whispers heard.

I was cautioned to look to this, and then we went on. The close of the scene was a bustling one, and the stage manager explained it thus:

'You' (the landlord) 'put the lantern close to my face, when you say "Tis he!" I

'You all cower down.'

spring up, throwing down the table' (a stamp here to emphasize this). 'I knock you down. You two try to seize me; I break from you, and throw you down, and cross centre' (doing so). 'I gain door, open it, and stand there, pointing revolver. You all cower down.' We were squatting on our toes, as an acknowledgment of having been all bowled over like a set of nine-pins – or rather four-pins in our case – and we now further bobbed our heads, to show that we did cower.

'Picture,' says the stage manager approvingly, as drop falls. 'Hurried music all through that, Mr P. Mind you all keep well up the stage' ('up' the stage means towards the back, and 'down' the stage, consequently, implies near the footlights) 'so as to let the drop come down. What front drops have you got? Have you got an interior? We want a cottage interior.' This latter was spoken to a stage carpenter, who was dragging some flats about. Do not be shocked, gentle reader; a stage flat is a piece of scenery. No other kind of flat is even seen on the stage.

'I dunno,' answered the man. 'Where's Jim? Jim!'

It appeared that Jim had just stepped outside for a minute. He came back at that point, however, wiping his mouth, and greatly indignant at hearing the sound of his own name.

'All right, all right,' was his wrathful comment, as he came up the yard; 'don't sing it; he ain't dead. What the devil's the matter? Is the 'ouse a-fire? *You* never go out, do yer!'

Jim was the head carpenter, and was a sulky and disagreeable man, even for a stage carpenter. When he wasn't 'just stepped outside for a minute,' he was quarrelling inside, so that instead of anybody's objecting to his frequent temporary retirements, his absence was rather welcomed. He, in common with all stage carpenters, held actors and actresses in the greatest contempt, as people who were always in the way, and without whom the play would get on much better. The chief charm about him, however, was his dense stupidity. This trait was always brought into particular prominence whenever the question of arranging scenery was under discussion.

Fresh scenery is a very great rarity at the minor theatres. When anything very special is produced, and an unusually long run is expected, say, of a month or six weeks, one or two scenes may, perhaps, be specially painted, but, as a rule, reliance is placed upon the scenery, the gradual growth of years, already in stock, which, with a little alteration, and a good deal of make-shift, generally does duty for the 'entirely new and elaborate scenery' so minutely described in the posters. Of course, under these circumstances, slight inconsistencies must be put up with. Nobody objects to a library drop representing ''tween decks of the *Sarah Jane*,' or to a back parlour being called a banqueting hall. This is to be expected. Our stage manager was not a narrow-minded man on the subject of accessories. He would have said nothing about such things as these. He himself had, on the occasion of one of his benefits, played *Hamlet* with nothing but one 'interior' and 'a garden,' and he had been a member of a fit-up company that travelled with a complete Shakespearian *répertoire* and four set scenes; so that he was not likely to be too exacting. But even *he* used to be staggered at Jim's ideas of mounting. Jim's notion of a 'distant view of Hampstead Heath by moonlight,' was either a tropical island, or the backing of an old transformation scene; and for any place in London – no matter what, whether Whitechapel or St James's Park – he invariably suggested a highly realistic representation of Waterloo Bridge in a snow-storm.

In the present instance, on being asked for the cottage interior, he let down a log cabin, with a couple of bowie knives and revolvers artistically arranged over the fire-place; anticipating any doubt upon the subject of suitableness by an assurance that, there you were, and you couldn't do better than that. The objection, that a log cabin with bowie knives and revolvers over the fire-place, though it was doubtless a common enough object in the Australian bush or the backwoods of America, was never, by any chance, found in England, and that the cottage to be represented was supposed to be within a few miles of London, he considered as too frivolous to need comment, and passed it over in silent contempt. Further argument had the effect of raising up Jim's stock authority, a certain former lessee, who had been dead these fifteen years, and about whom nobody else but Jim seemed to have the faintest recollection. It appeared that this gentleman had always used the log cabin scene for English cottages, and Jim guessed that *he* (the defunct lessee) knew what he was about, even if he (Jim) was a fool. The latter of Jim's suppositions had never been disputed, and it was a little too late then to discuss the former. All I can say is, that if Jim's Mr Harris – as this mysterious manager was generally dubbed – really did mount his productions in the manner affirmed, their effect must have been novel in the extreme.

Nothing could induce Jim to shew anything else that morning, although the manager reminded him of a cottage scene having been expressly painted for the last lessee. Jim didn't know where it was. Besides, one of the ropes was broken, and it couldn't be got at then. After which little brush with the enemy, he walked away, and took up a row with the gas man at the very point where he had dropped it twenty minutes before.

Scenery and props were not being used at this, the first, rehearsal, the chief object of which was merely to arrange music, extrances and exits, and general business; but of course it was desirable to know as soon as possible what scenery was available, and whether it required any altering or repairing.

In the second scene the leading lady made her first appearance, an event which called forth all the energies of the orchestra. It would not do for her to burst upon the audience all at once. Great and sudden joy is dangerous. They must be gradually prepared for it. Care was exercised that the crisis should be well led up to, and that she should appear exactly at the right moment. When all was satisfactorily settled, the cue was announced to her by the stage manager. He said it was, 'Pom-pom – pom-pom – pom-pom – pom – POM – POM.'

'That's your cue, my dear.'

On the stage, everybody calls the actresses, 'My dear'. You soon pick it up, especially in the case of the young and pretty ones.

'Where do I come on from?' asked the leading lady.

'I can't say, my dear, until I've seen the drop. There'll most likely be a door in it, and then you can come on from the back.'

Entrances from the back, it may be remarked, are the favourite ones. Indeed, some artistes will seldom come on from anywhere else. Of course, you make a much better impression on an audience, as regards first appearance, by facing them on your entrance and walking straight down towrds them, than by coming on sideways and then turning round. Entrances from the back, however, are sometimes carried to excess, and a whole scene is rendered unnatural and absurd, merely to gratify personal vanity.

I will finish what I have to say about

'You can come on from the back.'

this rehearsal by giving a verbatim report of a small part of it; viz.: the fourth scene of the first act. The actual scene is this:

STAGE MANAGER, *standing* CENTRE *with his back to the footlights. Close behind him, perched in a high chair, the* LEADER OF THE BAND *solus, representing the orchestra with a fiddle. Two or three groups of artistes, chatting at the wings.* THE HEAVY MAN, *pacing up and down at the back, conning his part in an undertone, and occasionally stopping to suit the action to the word.* LOW COMEDY *and* WALKING GENT., *going through scene by themselves in* L. 3. E. SINGING CHAMBERMAID, *flirting with* JUVEN-ILES *(only one of them),* R. 2. E. PROPERTY MAN, *behind, making a veal and ham pie out of an old piece of canvas and a handful of shavings.* COUPLE OF CARPENTERS, *in white jackets, hovering about, with hammers in their hands, and mischief in their eyes, evidently on the look out for an excuse to make a noise.* CALL BOY *all over the place, and always in the way – except when wanted.*

OUR FIRST OLD MAN (*standing* R.C., *and reading his part by the aid of a very large pair of specs*). "'Er-er – wind howls – er-er-er – night as this, fifteen years ago – er – sweet child – er-r-r – stolen away – er-r-r – baby prattle – er-ears – er-r – shall I never hear her voice again?'"

He looks up, and finding that nobody makes any sign of caring a hang whether he does or not, he repeats the question louder.

STAGE MANAGER (*severely, as if this was a question that really must be answered*). "'Shall I never hear her voice again?" Oh! that's a music cue, Mr P. Have you got it down? Miss ——' (*stage name of the manager's wife*) 'sings a song there, without.'

MR P. 'No, I'll put it down now. What is it – "hear her voice again?"' (*Writes on some loose slips of paper, lying before him on the stage.*) 'Have you the music?'

STAGE MAN. 'Oh, anything dismal does. No matter what it is, so long as it gives 'em the hump. What will you have, my dear?'

MANAGER'S WIFE (*who has just finished a social bottle of Bass with another lady*). 'Oh, the old thing, you know. "Home, sweet home."'

JUVENILES (*in a whisper to* LOW COM.) 'Is *she* going to sing?'

William Telbin, set designer, in his studio

LOW COM. 'Yes, always does it.'

JUVENILES. 'Oh, my ——!'

MAN. WIFE *and* THE FIDDLE *do first verse of 'Home, sweet home'.*

FIRST OLD MAN. '"Ah, that voice – er-er – echo of old memories – er-er-er – houseless wanderer – dry herself"' (*crossing and opening an imaginary door*). '"Poor child – er-er-er – I'm an old man – er – my wife's out – return and – er – the homeless orphan."'

MAN. WIFE. 'Will there be any lime-light on here?'

FIRST OLD WOMAN (*sotto voce*). 'Oh, let her have some lime-light. She wants to let her back hair down.'

STAGE MAN. 'Certainly, my dear. There'll be a fire-place in this corner, and red lime-light from it.'

MAN. WIFE. 'Oh, all right; I only wanted to know. Now, what was it – "homeless orphan". Oh, that's my long speech, you know: "Is this a dream that I have dreamt before, – played here when a child."'

FIRST O. M. '"Sweet child – your face recalls strange memories of – er-er-er – been just your age."'

STAGE MAN. (*interrupting*). 'Slow music throughout.'

FIRST O. M. (*continuing*). '"Never from that night – er – golden – I can't believe she's dead."'

Scrape from the fiddle, followed by bar, to bring on FIRST OLD WOMAN.

FIRST O. W. (*without moving from her seat, and coming straight to the cue with a suddenness which startles everybody*). '"Fold you to my breast."'

MAN. WIFE. '"Mother!" – Got the rheumatism again?'

FIRST O. W. 'Got it *again*! It's never gone yet, drat it – "My child!"'

Powerful scrape from the fiddle.

FIRST O. M. 'Where am I?'

STAGE MAN. 'Left down stage.'

MAN. WIFE. 'We embrace, left centre. Knock heard.'

STAGE MAN. (*crossing centre*). 'That's me.★ Keep it up: it's a picture. You and Mrs —— there, embracing, and the old boy down in the corner, when I open the door. – Rain and wind for this scene, mind.'

★ That was the way he treated Lindley Murray. We were inexpressibly grieved and shocked – all of us – but what were we to do?

HOVERING CARPENTER (*at top of his voice*). 'Jim! wind and rain for last scene of first act.'

Husky but indignant voice from the flies, expressing an earnest desire that everyone should go to the devil.

STAGE MAN. (*who always rehearsed his speeches at full length, and in a tone of voice as if he were reciting the multiplication table*). '"I am pursued. My life is at stake. Hide me from these bloodhounds who are on my brack. Hark! they are here. Thank Heaven, they are past. I am safe. Ha, who is this we have here? 'Sdeath, I am in luck to night. Sir Henry will thank me, when I bring his strayed lamb back to him. Come with me my little runaway." Business. "Nay, resist not, or 'twill be the worse for all." I catch hold of you. We struggle. "Come, I say, with me. Come, I say."'

FIRST O. W. – '"Die together."'

Scrape from the fiddle.

STAGE MAN. (*loudly, after waiting a minute*). '"Die together."'

FIRST O. W. 'I beg pardon. I didn't hear.' (*Fumbles with his part, and loses his place.*)

MAN. WIFE. 'He really ought to use an ear-trumpet.'

FIRST O. W. '"Er-r-r – Heaven will give me strength – er – can strike a blow."' (*Shakes his stick at* STAGE MANAGER.)

Tremendous hammering suddenly begun at back, eliciting forcible expressions of disapproval from all the members of the company, with the exception of the FIRST OLD MAN, *who doesn't hear it, and goes on calmly with the rehearsal all by himself.*

STAGE MAN. (*in a rage*). 'Stop that noise! Stop that noise, I say!'

Noise continues.

JIM (*eager for the fray*). 'How can we do our work without noise, I should like to know?'

STAGE MAN. (*crossly*). 'Can't you do it at some other time?'

JIM (*angrily*). 'No, we can't do it at some other time! Do you think we're here all night?'

STAGE MAN. (*mildly*). 'But, my dear fellow, how can we go on with the rehearsal?'

JIM (*in a rage*). 'I don't know anything about you and your rehearsal! That's not my business, is it? I do my own work; I don't do other people's work! I don't want to be told how to do my work!'

(*Pours forth a flood of impassioned eloquence for the next ten minutes, during which time the hammering is also continued. Complete collapse of* STAGE MANAGER, *and suspension of rehearsal. Subsequent dryness on the part of* JIM.)

MAN. WIFE (*when rehearsal is at last resumed*). 'Just try back that last bit, will you, for positions?'

The last two or three movements gone over again.

Then:

STAGE MAN. 'We all three struggle towards door. "Stand back, old man! I do not wish to harm thee!" – I push you aside. "Back or it will be murder!" – This must be well worked up. "Who dares to stay me?" (*to* LOW COMEDY). 'There'll be a bar to bring you on. You know the business.'

LOW COM. (*coming forward*). '"Shure and *I* will."'

Scrape from fiddle.

STAGE MAN. 'Well, then there's our struggle.' (STAGE MAN-AGER *and* LOW COMEDY *take hold of each other's shoulders, and turn round.*) 'I'll have the book in the left-hand side.'

LOW COM. '"Ah, begorra, shure he's clane gone; but, be jabers, I've got this"' (*holding up an imaginary pocket- book*), '"and its worth a precious deal more than he is."'

STAGE MAN. 'End of first act. – Tommy, go and fetch me half a pint of stout.'

CHAPTER 6

Scenery and Supers

WE HAD FIVE rehearsals for this play.

'What the dickens do they want with so many?' was the indignant comment of the First Old Woman. 'Why, they'll rehearse it more times than they'll play it.'

I thought five a ridiculously small number at the time, especially when I remembered my amateur days, and the thirty or so rehearsals, nearly all full-dress ones, required for a short farce; but there came a time when I looked upon two as betokening extraordinary anxiety about a production. In the provinces, I have known a three-act comedy put on without any rehearsal at all, and with half the people not even knowing the patter. 'Business' was arranged in whispered consultations, while the play was pro- ceeding, and when things got into a more than usually glorious muddle, one or other of

Working drops and borders from the First Fly Gallery, 1888

the characters would come off the stage and have a look at the book. As for the prompter, after vainly struggling to keep them to one act at a time, and to dissuade the hero from making love to the wrong girl, he came to the conclusion that he was only in the way, and so went and had a quiet pipe at the stage door, and refrained from worrying himself further.

The rehearsals got more ship-shape as we went on. At the fourth, every one was supposed to be 'letter perfect,' and 'parts' were tabooed. On this occasion, the piece was played straight through with nothing omitted, and the orchestra (two fiddles, a bass-viol, cornet, and drum) appeared in full force. For the last rehearsal, props and scenery were called. We had an exciting time with Jim, over the scenery, as might be expected. He had a row with everybody, and enjoyed himself immensely.

'Half an hour was quite long enough for him to turn a hay-field into a churchyard.'

I saw our scene painter then for the first time. He was a jolly little fellow, and as full of cheery contrivance as a Mark Tapley. No difficulties seemed to daunt him. If a court of justice were wanted for the following night, and the nearest thing he had to it was a bar parlour, he was not in the least dismayed. He would have the bar parlour down; paint in a bit here; paint out a bit there; touch up a bit somewhere else – there was your court of justice! Half an hour was quite long enough for him to turn a hay-field into a churchyard, or a prison into a bedroom.

There was only one want, in the present case, that he didn't supply, and that was cottages. All the virtuous people in the play lived in cottages. I never saw such a run on cottages. There were plenty of other residences to which they would have been welcome – halls, palaces, and dungeons, the saloon cabin of a P. and O. steamer, drawing-room of No. 200, Belgrave Square (a really magnificent apartment this, with a clock on the mantelpiece). But no, they would all of them live in cottages. It would not pay to alter three or four different scenes, and turn them all into cottages, especially as they might, likely enough, be wanted for something else in a week's time; so our one cottage interior had to accommodate about four distinct families. To keep up appearances, however, it was called by a different name on each occasion. With a round table and a candle, it was a widow's cottage. With two candles and a gun, it was the blacksmith's house. A square table instead of a round one – 'Daddy Solomon's home on the road to London. "Home, sweet home".' Put a spade in the corner, and hang a coat behind the door, and you had the old mill on the Yorkshire moors.

It was all no use though. The audience, on the opening night, greeted its second appearance with cries of kindly recognition, and at once entered into the humour of the thing. A Surrey-side Saturday-night audience are generally inclined to be cheerful, and, if the fun on the stage doesn't satisfy them, they rely on their own resources. After one or two more appearances, the cottage became an established favourite with the gallery. So much so, indeed, that when two scenes passed without its being let down, there were many and anxious inquiries after it, and an earnest hope expressed that nothing serious had happened to it. Its reappearance in the next act (as something entirely new) was greeted with a round of applause, and a triumphant demand to know, 'Who said it was lost?'

It was not until the last rehearsal, that the supers were brought into play – or work, as they would have called it. These supers were drawn from two distinct sources. About half of them were soldiers, engaged to represent the military force of the drama, while the other half, who were to be desperate rioters, had been selected from among the gentry of the New Cut neighbourhood.

The soldiers, who came under the command of their sergeant, were by far the best thing in the play. They gave an air of reality to all the scenes in which they appeared. They *were* soldiers, and went about their business on the stage with the same calm precision that they would have displayed in the drill yard, and with as much seriousness as if they had been in actual earnest. When the order was given to 'fix bayonets and charge', they did so with such grim determination, that there was no necessity at all to direct the stage mob to 'feign fear and rush off L. I. E'. They went as one man, in a hurry. There was no trouble, either, about rehearsing the soldiers – no cursing and swearing required, which, in itself was an immense saving of time. The stage manager told the sergeant what was wanted. That gruff-voiced officer passed the order on to his men (first translating it into his own unintelligible lingo), and the thing was done.

To represent soldiers on the stage, real soldiers should, without doubt, be employed, but it is no good attempting to use them for anything else. They are soldier-like in everything they do. You may dress them up in what you choose, and call them what you will, but they will never be anything else but soldiers. On one occasion, our manager tried them as a rabble. They were carefully instructed how to behave. They were told how to rush wildly on with a fierce tumultuous yell; how to crowd together at the back of the stage, and, standing there, surging backwards and forwards like an angry sea, brandish their weapons, and scowl menacingly upon the opposing myrmidons of the law, until, at length, their sullen murmurs deepening into a roar of savage hate, they would break upon the wall of steel before them, and sweep it from their path, as pent-up waters, bursting their bonds, bear down some puny barrier.

That was the theory of the thing. That is how a stage mob *ought* to behave itself. How it really does behave itself is pretty generally known. It comes in with a jog-trot, every member of it prodding the man in front of him in the small of his back. It spreads itself out in a line across the stage and grins. When the signal is given for the rush, each man – still grinning – walks up to the soldier nearest to him, and lays hold of that warrior's gun. The two men then proceed to heave the murderous weapon slowly up and down, as if it were a pump handle. This they continue to do with steady perseverance, until the soldier, apparently from a fit of apoplexy – for there is no outward and visible cause whatever to account for it – suddenly collapses, when the conquering rioter takes the gun away from him, and entangles himself in it.

This is funny enough, but our soldiers made it funnier still. One might just as well have tried to get a modern House of Commons to represent a disorderly rabble. They simply couldn't do it. They went on in single file at the double quick, formed themselves into a hollow square in the centre of the stage, and then gave three distinct cheers, taking time from the sergeant. That was their notion of a rabble.

The other set, the regular bob (sometimes eighteen-pence) a-night 'sūps', were of a very different character. Professional supers, taken as a class, are the most utterly dismal specimens of humanity to be met with in this world. Compared with them, 'sandwich-men' are dashing and rollicky. Ours were no exception to the rule. They

hung about in a little group by themselves, and looked
such a picture of dejected dinginess, that their
mere presence had a depressing effect upon
everybody else. Strange that men can't be
gay and light-hearted on an income of six
shillings a week, but so it is.

One of them I must exclude from this
description – a certain harmless idiot,
who went by the title of 'Mad Mat,' though
he himself always gave his name as 'Mr
Matthew Alexander St George Clement.'

This poor fellow had been a super for a
good many years, but there had evidently
been a time when he had played a very
different part in life. 'Gentleman' was stamped
very plainly upon his thin face, and where he was
not crazy, he showed thought and education.
Rumour said that he had started life as a young
actor, full of promise and talent, but what had sent
him mad nobody knew. The ladies naturally attributed it
to love, it being a fixed tenet among the fair sex that
everything that happens to mankind, from finding themselves in
bed with their boots on to having the water cut off, is all owing to that tender passion.
On the other hand the uncharitable – generally a majority – suggested drink. But
nobody did anything more than conjecture: nobody really knew. The link between the
prologue and the play was lost. Mat himself was under the firm conviction that he was
a great actor, who was only kept from appearing in the leading *rôles* by professional
jealously. But a time would come, and then he would show us what he could do.
Romeo was his great ambition. One of these days he meant to act that character. He
had been studying it for years, he once whispered me in confidence, and when he
appeared in it, he knew he should make a sensation.

Strange to say, his madness did not interfere at all with his superial duties. While on
the stage, he was docile enough, and did just as he saw the other supers do. It was only
off the stage that he put on his comically pathetic dignity: then, if the super-master

THEATRE ROYAL,

KING STREET, BRISTOL.

Lessee and Director   -   -   -   A. MELVILLE, Queen Square.

EXTRA WEEK !
RE-OPEN AT SHORT NOTICE
MONDAY, JULY 15th and During the Week.

MONDAY, July 15, FOR SIX NIGHTS ONLY

SPECIAL PRODUCTION OF

THE NOBLE
VAGABOND

The Startling Realistic Melodrama, from the

PRINCESS'S THEATRE, LONDON,

As played with Enormous Success for over 200 Nights,

SUPPORTED BY A POWERFUL COMPANY

UNDER THE DIRECTION OF

Mr. GILBERT VERNON

BY ARRANGEMENT WITH

Mr. JOSEPH ROWLAND

SPECIAL ENGAGEMENT OF

Mrs. AUGUSTUS BRIGHT

The Piece produced under the supervision of Mr. Charles Warner and the Author

Business Manager ...	... ⎫ For ⎧ ...	Mr. HARRY LYNDON
Stage Manager ...	... ⎭ Mr. ROWLAND ⎩ ...	Mr. GEORGE IRWIN

TAYLOR BROS., Broad Weir, Bristol.

attempted to tell him what to do, he would make a ceremonious bow, and observe, with some hauteur, that Mr St George Clement was not accustomed to be instructed how to act his part. He never mixed with the other supers, but would stand apart, talking low to himself, and seeming to see something a long way off. He was the butt of the whole theatre, and his half-timid, half-pompous ways afforded us a good deal of merriment; but sometimes there was such a sad look in Mat's white face, that it made one's heart ache more than one's sides.

His strange figure and vague history haunted my thoughts in a most uncomfortable manner. I used to think of the time when those poor vacant eyes looked out upon the world, full of hope and ambition, and then I wondered if *I* should ever become a harmless idiot, who thought himself a great actor.

CHAPTER 7

Dressing

WE HAD NO dress rehearsals. In the whole course of my professional life, I remember but one dress rehearsal. That was for a pantomime in the provinces. Only half the costumes arrived in time for it. I myself appeared in a steel breast-plate and helmet, and a pair of check trousers; and I have a recollection of seeing somebody else – the King of the Cannibal Islands, I think – going about in spangled tights and a frock coat. There was a want of finish, as one might say, about the affair.

Old stagers, of course, can manage all right without them, but the novice finds it a little awkward to jump from plain dress rehearsals to the performance itself. He has been making love to a pale-faced, middle-aged lady, dressed in black grenadine and a sealskin jacket, and he is quite lost when smiled upon by a high-complexioned, girlish young thing, in blue silk stockings and short skirts. He finds defying stout, good-tempered Mr Jones a very different thing to bullying a bettle-browed savage, of appearance something between Bill Sykes and a Roman gladiator, and whose acquaintance he then makes for the first time. Besides, he is not at all sure that he has got hold of the right man.

I, in my innocence, so fully expected at least one dress rehearsal, that, when time went on, and there were no signs of any such thing, I mooted the question myself, so that there should be no chance of its being accidentally overlooked. The mere idea, however, was scouted. It was looked upon as the dream of a romantic visionary.

'Don't talk about dress rehearsals, my

Dress rehearsal for a pantomime in the provinces

boy,' was the reply; 'think yourself lucky if you get your dress all right by the night.'

The 'my boy,' I may remark, by no means implied that the speaker thought me at all youthful. Indeed, seeing that I was eighteen at the time, it hardly could, you know. Every actor is 'my boy,' just, as before mentioned, every actress is 'my dear.' At first I was rather offended; but when I heard grey-headed stars, and respectable married leads, addressed in the same familiar and unceremonious manner, my dignity recovered itself. It is well our dignity is not as brittle as Humpty Dumpty. How very undignified we should all become, before we had been long in this world.

As a matter of fact, nobody – at all events, none of the men, with the exception of Chequers – seemed to care in the slightest about what they should wear. 'Chequers' was the name we had given to our walking gentleman, as a delicate allusion to the pattern of his overcoat. I think I have already described the leading features in this young man's private-life apparel. He went in a good deal for dress, and always came out strong. His present ambition was to wear his new ulster in the piece, and this he did, though, seeing that the action of the play was supposed to take place a century ago, it was hardly consistent with historical accuracy. But then historical accuracy was not a strong point with our company, who went more on the principle of what you happened to have by you. At the better class of London theatre, everything is now provided by the management, and the actor has only to put on what is given him. But with the theatres and companies into which I went, things were very different; costumes being generally left to each person's individual discretion. For ordinary modern-dress parts, we had to use our own things entirely, and in all cases we were expected to find ourselves in hosiery and boot leather, by which I mean such things as tights and stockings, and the boots and shoes of every period and people; the rest of the costume was provided for us – at all events in London.

In the provinces, where every article necessary for either a classical tragedy or a pantomime has often to be found by the actor himself, I have seen some very remarkable wardrobe effects. A costume play, under these circumstances, rivalled a fancy dress ball in variety. It was considered nothing out of the way for a father, belonging to the time of George III, to have a son who evidently, from his dress, flourished in the reign of Charles II. As for the supers, when there were any, they were attired in the first thing that came to hand, and always wore their own boots.

Picturesqueness was the great thing. Even now and at some of the big London houses, this often does duty for congruity and common sense. The tendency to regard all female foreigners as Italian peasant girls, and to suppose that all agricultural labourers wear red waist-coats embroidered with yellow, still lingers on the stage.

Even where costumes were provided, the leading actors, and those who had well-stocked wardrobes of their own, generally preferred to dress the part themselves, and there was nobody who did not supplement the costumer's ideas to some greater or less extent.

I am speaking only of the men. Actresses nearly always find their own dresses. There is no need of a very varied wardrobe in their case, for in spite of all the talk about female fashions, a woman's dress is much the same now as in the time of the Mrs Noahs – at least, so it seems to me, judging from my own ark. The dress that Miss Eastlake wore in the *Silver King* would, I am sure, do all right for Ophelia; and what difference is there between Queen Elizabeth and Mrs Bouncer? None whatever, except about the collar and sleeves; and anybody can alter a pair of sleeves and make a ruff. Why do actresses have so many dresses! As far as mere shape is concerned, one would do for everything, with a few slight alterations. You just tack on a tuck or a furbelow, or take in a flounce, and you are.

Maybe I'm wrong, though.

We were told to look in at the costumier's some time during the week, for him to take our measurements, and those of us who were inexperienced in theatrical costumiers did so, and came away with the hopeful idea that we were going to be sent clothes that would nearly fit us. The majority, however, did not go through s farce, but quietly took what they found in their dressing-rooms on the opening night, and squeezed themselves into, or padded themselves out to it, as the necessity happened to be.

The dressing-rooms (two rows of wooden sheds, divided by a narrow passage) were situate over the property room, and were reached by

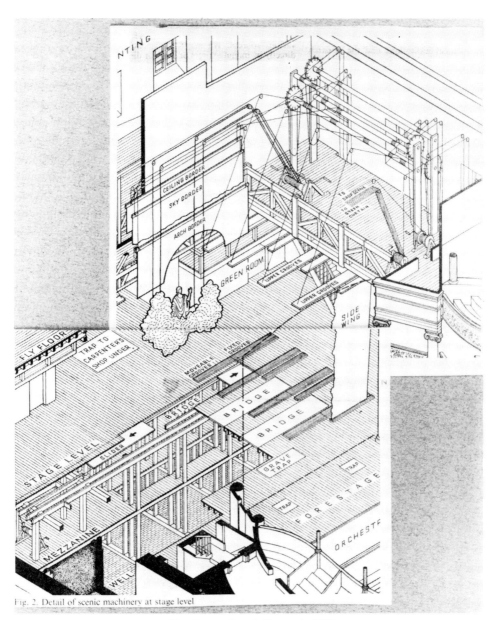

Fig. 2. Detail of scenic machinery at stage level

The Theatre Royal, Plymouth, 1811

means of a flight of steps, which everybody ascended and descended very gingerly indeed, feeling sure each time that the whole concern would come down before they got to the other end. These apartments had been carefully prepared for our reception. The extra big holes in the partitions had been bunged up with brown paper, and the whitewash had been laid on everywhere with a lavishness that betokened utter disregard of the expense; though as, before a week was over, nearly the whole of it had been transferred to our clothes, this was rather a waste, so far as the management was concerned. It was even reported that one of the rooms had been swept out, but I never saw any signs of such a thing having been done myself either then or at any other time, and am inclined to look upon the statement merely in the light of a feeler, thrown out for the purpose of getting at the views of the charwoman. If so, however, it was a failure. She said nothing on hearing it, but looked offended, and evidently considered it a subject that should not have been mentioned to a lady.

One or two of the doors still hung upon their hinges, and could, with a little manoeuvring, be opened or shut: but in most cases they had been wrenched off, and stood propped up against their own posts, like drunken revellers taken home by the cabman. The only means therefore, of getting in or out of the rooms was by lifting them bodily away. It was a pretty sight to watch some stout, short-winded actor, staggering about the place with one of these great

doors in his arms, trying to make it stand up.
After a series of fearful efforts, he would
get it wedged firmly across the passage,
and, at that exact moment, some one
would be sure to come rushing upstairs
in a desperate hurry to get to his room.
He could not, of course, pass while the
wretched door was in that position, so,
with a view of expediting matters, he
would lay hold of the other side of it, and
begin tugging. The first man, not being
able to see what was going on, and
thinking larks were being played with
him, would plunge about more wildly
than ever, and jam the door down on the
other fellow's toes. Then they would both
grapple madly with it, one on each side,
bump each other's heads with it, crush

each other with it against the sides of the passage, and end by all three going down in a
heap together, the door uppermost.

The furniture provided, simple though it was, had evidently been selected with a
thoughtful desire that everything should be in keeping: it consisted of a few broken
chairs. The supply of toilet requisites in hand, too, seemed to be rather limited, but
great care and ingenuity had been displayed in their distribution. There not being
enough basins and jugs to go all round, these had been divided. Some rooms had a jug
but no basin, while others had a basin but no jug, either circumstance being a capital
excuse for leaving them without any water. Where there was neither basin nor jug, you
could safely reckon on a soap dish. We were supplied with towels, the allowance being
one a fortnight – a small thin one with a big hole in the middle – amongst six, but we
brought our own soap; at least some of us did, and the others, without a moment's
hesitation, appropriated it.

One of the rooms was better appointed than the others, being able to boast a
washstand, made out of an old cane chair that had lost its back and one of its legs. This
article of luxury was the cause of a good deal of bitterness at first among the occupants

of the less favoured apartments, but its tendency towards
sudden and unexpected collapse soon lessened this feeling of
envy. Even its owners ceased to take any pride in it, after a
while, and it was eventually kicked to pieces in a fit of
frenzy by Juveniles; it having been the cause, as far as we
could gather from his disjointed blasphemy, of his being
compelled to play all the rest of that evening in sopping wet
tights.

A blear-eyed individual used to hang about these rooms of
a night. He called himself a dresser, though, for all the
dressing he ever did, he might just as well have been a kitchen
one. He got a dressing himself once for upsetting a pot of
paint over Jim's supper; but that was the only one he ever, to
my knowledge, assisted at. However, he came in handy to
go out for sheep's head and porter.

But although the dressing-rooms surprised me somewhat, they did not disappoint me. I had built no expectations
upon them. I had conjured up no airy
visions concerning them. Mine eyes had
not hungered to gaze upon their imagined
glories. No, the dressing-rooms I bore up under; it
was the green room that crushed me. It was about the green room that my brightest
hopes had been centred. It was there that I was to flirt with Beauty, and converse with
Intellect. I had pictured a brilliantly lighted and spacious apartment with a polished oak
floor, strewn with costly rugs; gilded walls, hung with the choicest gems of art; and a
lofty, painted ceiling. There would be luxurious easy-chairs and couches, upon which
to rest ourselves between our artistic labours; a piano, from which fairy fingers would
draw forth rapturous strains, while I turned over the music; and carved cabinets, filled
with old china, and other rare and precious nicknacks. Heavy curtains, over the door,
would deaden the outside din to a droning murmur, which would mingle pleasantly
with the low hum of cheerful conversation within; whilst the flickering fire-light,
flashing upon the Spanish mahogany furniture, and glittering reflected in the many
mirrors round the room, would throw a touch of homeliness over what might

otherwise have been the almost too dazzling splendour of the place.

There was no green room. There never had been a green room. I never saw a green room, except in a play, though I was always on the look out for it. I met an old actor once who had actually been in one, and I used to get him to come and tell me all about it. But even his recollections were tinged with a certain vagueness. He was not quite sure whether it had been at Liverpool or at Newcastle that he had come across it, and at other times he thought it must have been at Exeter. But wherever it was, the theatre had been burnt down a good many years ago – about that he was positive.

On one occasion, I went specially to a big London theatre where, I was assured, there really was one, and it cost me four-and-sevenpence in drinks. I found the green room all right, but they said I had better not go in, because it was chock full of properties, and I might break something in the dark.

The truth is that where a green room was originally provided, it has been taken by the star or the manager, as his or her private room, and the rest of the company are left to spend their off time either in their own dressing-rooms, where they are always in each other's way, or at the wings, where they catch cold, and are hustled by the scene-shifters.

'At the wings, where they catch cold.'

CHAPTER 8

My 'First Deboo'

O N SATURDAY CAME the opening night, and with it my first appearance before the British public – my 'first deboo' as our perruquier called it. In thinking about it beforehand, I had been very much afraid lest I should be nervous; but strange to say, I never experienced stage-fright at any time. I say strange, because, at that period of my life at all events, I was – as true greatness generally is – of a modest and retiring disposition. In my very early youth, I believe, I was not so. I am told that in my frock and pinafore days, I used to stand upon the table, and recite poetry, to the intense gratification of my elderly relatives (ah, the old folks knew how to enjoy themselves when I was a boy!); and an old nurse of mine always insisted that on one occasion I collected half a crown in an omnibus by my spirited rendering of 'Baa, baa, black sheep.' I have no recollection of this performance myself though, and, if it really did take place, where's the money? This part of the question has never, to my mind, been satisfactorily cleared up.

But however self-possessed I may have been at eight, I was anything but so at eighteen. Even now, I would not act to a drawing room full of people for a thousand pounds – supposing the company considered the effort worth that sum. But before a public audience, I was all right, and entirely free from that shyness about which, in private life, my lady friends so bitterly complain. I could not see the people for one thing – at all events, not those beyond the third row of stalls. The blaze of light surrounding one on the stage, and the dimness of the rest of the house, give the audience a shadowy and ghost-like appearance, and make it impossible to see more than a general mass of white faces. As I never

Modern ghost-raising: a sketch behind the scenes at the London Polytechnic, January 1875

noticed the 'hundreds upon hundreds of glaring eyes,' they did not trouble me, and I let 'em glare. The most withering glance in the world won't crush a blind man.

If I had been nervous on the first night, I think I should have had a good excuse for it, knowing, as I did, that a select party of my most particular friends, including a few medical students and clergymen's sons, were somewhere in the theatre; having come down in a body with the intention of giving me a fair start, as they said. They had insisted on coming. I had begged them not to trouble themselves on my account, but they wouldn't hear of it. They said it would be such a comfort to me to know that they were there. That was their thoughtful kindness. It touched me.

I said: 'Look here, you know, if you fellows are going to play the fool, I'll chuck the whole blessed thing up.'

They said they were not going to play the fool: they were coming to see me. I raised no further objections.

But I checkmated them. I lied to those confiding young men with such an air of simple truthfulness, that they believed me, though they had known me for years. Even now, after all this time, I feel a glow of pride when I think how consummately I deceived them. They knew nothing of the theatres or actors over the water, so I just gave them the name of our first old man, and told them that that was the name I had taken. I exaggerated the effect of making-up, and impressed upon them the idea that I should be so changed that they would never believe that it was I; and I requested them especially to note my assumed voice. I did not say what character I was going to play, but I let slip a word now and then implying that my mind was running on grey hairs and long-lost children, and I bought a stick exactly similar to the one the poor old gentleman was going to use in the part, and let it lie about.

So far as I was concerned the plan was a glorious success, but the effect upon the old man was remarkable. He was too deaf to hear exactly what was going on, but he gathered enough to be aware that he was the object of a certain amount of attention, and that he was evidently giving great satisfaction to a portion of the audience; which latter circumstance apparently surprised him. The dear fellows gave him a splendid reception when he first appeared. They applauded everything he said or did throughout the play, and called for him after every act. They encored his defiance of the villain, and, when he came on without his hat in a snow scene, they all pulled out their handkerchiefs and sobbed aloud. At the end they sent a message round to tell him to hurry up, as they were waiting for him at the stage door, an announcement that had

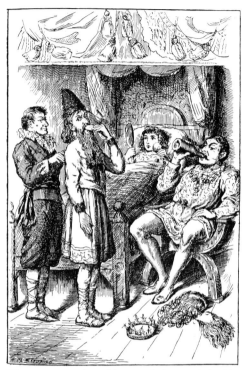

'The premature rise of the curtain is attended with
. . . ludicrous results.'

the effect of sending him out by the front way in wonderfully quick time.

On the whole that first night passed off pretty well. First nights are trying times at all theatres. The state of excitement behind the scenes is at fever heat, and the stage manager and the head carpenter become positively dangerous. In sensation pieces, where the author plays second fiddle to the scene-shifter, this, of course, is especially the case.

Now – as all modern playgoers know – there are never any hitches or delays on first nights. At all events, not at any of the West-end houses, where everything is always a 'triumph of stage management!' But in my time, hitches on first nights were the rule rather than the exception, and, when a scene was got through without any special mishap, we felt we were entitled to shake hands with one another.

I remember one first night at a London theatre where the sensation was to be the fall of a house, crushing the villain (*literally*) at the end of the fourth act. Great expectations were entertained about this 'effect.' It was confidently calculated that the collapse of this building would bring down the house, and so no doubt it would have done, if, owing to a mistake in the cues, the curtain had not come down first. The house fell beautifully, the dummy villain was killed on the spot, and the heroine saved in the nick of time by the hero (who, in these plays, is always just round the corner), but the audience only wondered what all the noise was about, and why no one had struck an attitude at the end of the act.

But however flat things fell in front, the sensation behind was undoubted. When the excitement had partially subsided, there was an energetic inquiry for the man who had let down the curtain, but it appeared that he had left without stopping even to put on his hat. This did not transpire at the time, however, and, for half an hour afterwards, the manager was observed to be wandering about with a crowbar, apparently looking for someone.

The premature rise of the curtain is attended with still more ludicrous results. On one occasion, I call to mind, the 'rag' went up unexpectedly, and discovered the following scene:

> The king of the country, sitting by the side of his dying son. He is drinking beer out of a bottle.
> His wig and beard lie beside him on the floor.——
> The dying son, touching herself up by the aid of a powder-puff and a hand-glass. –
> The chief priest of the country (myself) eating a Bath bun, while a friendly super buttons him up the back.

Another time I recollect was at a very small provincial theatre. There was only one dressing room in the whole place, and that the ladies had of course. We men had to dress on the stage itself. You can imagine the rest – the yell, the confusion; the wild stampede; the stage looking like the south bank of the Serpentine after 8 p.m.; the rapid descent of the curtain; the enthusiastic delight of the audience. It was the greatest success we had during our stay.

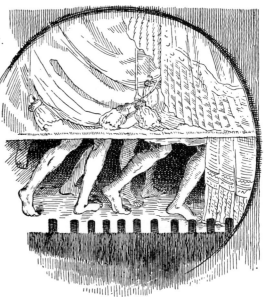

I have a strong opinion, however, that this latter catastrophe was not due so much to accident as to a certain mean villain among the company, whose name, in consideration of his family, I refrain from mentioning.

CHAPTER 9

Birds of Prey

REMAINED IN London with my first manager during the whole summer season, which lasted about nine months, and I think that, altogether, it was the happiest period of my stage career. The company was a thoroughly agreeable one. It was a genial, jovial company – a 'Here you are, my boy; just in time for a pull' sort of company – a 'Hail fellow well met' with everybody else sort of company. Among players there are none of those caste distinctions such as put an insurmountable barrier between the man who sells coal by the ton and the man who sells it by the hundredweight. 'The Profession' is a Republic. Lead and Utility walk about arm-in-arm, and the Star and the Singing Chambermaid drink out of the same pewter. We were all as friendly and sociable together as brothers and sisters – perhaps even more so – and the evening spent in those bare dressing rooms was the pleasantest part of the day. There was never a dull moment, but always plenty of bustle and fun, plenty of anecdotes, plenty of good stories – ah, they could tell 'em! – plenty of flirting, and talking and joking, and laughing.

What jolly little suppers they were, too, brought in smoking hot from the cook-shop over the way, and in the middle of which we had to be constantly rushing off with our mouths full to rescue some unfortunate female who was always getting into trouble, or to murder an uncle; and how wide we had to open our lips, when eating, lest

THEATRE ROYAL, BRISTOL.

Monday, April 17th, and during Week (Good Friday excepted).

THE GIRL WHO LOST HER CHARACTER

BY WALTER MELVILLE

THEATRE ROYAL, BRISTOL.   Monday, April 17th, during Week (Good Friday excepted).

we should rub the carmine off! How delic-
ious a quart of six ale was after a row with
the police, or a struggle with the
man who had carried off the
girl! How enjoyable a smoke
when you had to hide your pipe
in your boot each time you heard a
foot-step, because smoking was
strictly prohibited!

I was not so contented at first as I might
have been. I expected about three pounds a
week salary after giving my one month gratis,
and I did not get it. My agreement it may be
remembered, stipulated that I should receive a
'salary according to ability' at the end of that time,
but the manager said he did not think there would
ever be enough money in the house to pay me at
that scale, and suggested nine shillings a week
instead, generously giving me the option of either
taking it or leaving it. I took it.

I took it because I saw plainly enough that if I
didn't I should get nothing, that he could find
twenty other young fellows as good as I to come
without any salary at all, and that the agreement
was not worth the paper it was written on. I was
wrath at the time, but, seeing that the nine shillings was soon raised to twelve, and
afterwards to fifteen and eighteen, I had really, taking things as they were, nothing to
grumble at; and, when I came to know a little more about professional salaries, and
learnt what even the old hands were glad to get I was very well satisfied.

The company was engaged at summer prices, which are a good deal less than winter
ones, and these latter average something less than the wages of an industrious sweep.
The public, who read of this actor receiving a hundred and twenty pounds a night, of
that actress making eight hundred pounds a week, of a low comedian's yearly income
being somewhere about six thousand pounds, and of a London manager who has

actually paid his rates and taxes (so he says), can scarcely have any idea of what existence at the bottom of the stage ladder is like. It is a long ladder, and there are very few who possess a personal experience at both ends. Those who do, however, must appreciate the contrast. Mr Henry Irving, speaking somewhere of his early days, mentions his weekly salary, I think, as having been twenty-five shillings; and no doubt at the time, he thought that very good, and can most likely remember when he got less. In the provinces, thirty shillings is a high figure for a good all-round 'respons-ibles,' and for that amount he is expected to be equal to Othello or Sir Peter Teazle at a moment's notice, and to find his own dress. A 'lead' may get three pounds in the winter, and a young 'utility' thinks himself very well off indeed on a guinea. Now and again, the latter will get twenty-two or -three shillings, but this only leads him into habits of extravagance, and he suffers for it afterwards. At the minor London theatres, there being no expenses connected with travelling, etc., the salaries are even less, and from eighteen shillings to two pounds are about the sums *promised*.

I do not believe I should ever have got even the salary I did, if it had not been for the extraordinary circumstance of a really successful season, so successful, indeed, that the fact could not be disguised, and, for the last three or four months – excess of good fortune having evidently turned the manager's head – salaries were paid *regularly and in full!* This is not romancing, it is plain, sober truth. Such a thing may surprise my readers, especially those who know much about the stage, but it cannot surprise them one fiftieth part so much as it surprised us. It completely bewildered the majority of the company. To have anything more than five shillings paid to them at one time seemed to confuse them and, on treasury days, they went away from the theatre with a puzzled air of affluence and responsibility.

They had not been accustomed to receiving salaries in that way. What they had been used to was, say, two-and-sixpence one day, sixpence at the beginning of the next night, another twopence after the first act, and eightpence as they were going away.

'That makes one-and-four you've had to-night, and two-and-sixpence last night makes three-and-ten, mind.'

'Yes, but, hang it all, you know, there was four shillings owing from last week, and five-and-sixpence from the week before, that I've never had yet.'

'My dear boy, for Heaven's sake don't talk about last week and the week before. Do let's keep to one week at a time. We can't go back to the Flood.'

They had been accustomed to haggle and fight for every penny they got; to dodge and trick and bully for their money in a way that a sixty-per-cent money-lender would rather lose principal and interest than resort to; to entreat and clamour for it like Italian beggar children; to hang about after the acting manager like hungry dogs after a cat's-meat man; to come down to the theatre early in the morning and wait all day for him; to watch outside his room by the hour together, so as to rush in the moment the door was opened, and stick there till he threw them a shilling; to lie in wait at dark corners and spring out upon him as he passed; to run after him up stairs and down stairs; to sneak after him into public-house bars; or to drive him into a corner and threaten to punch his head unless he gave them another sixpence – this last expedient, of course, being possible only when the actor was big and the acting manager little. Fortunately acting managers mostly were little, otherwise the profession would have died of starvation.

If, as sometimes happened, they left the acting manager alone and went for the lessee himself, the latter would always refer them to the former, assuming for himself a magnificent indifference about such trivial things as money matters; and he would even play out the farce to the length of sending for the acting manager, and begging that gentleman, as a personal favour to himself, to let Mr So-and-So be paid without further delay, which the acting manager would gravely promise should be done.

If it had not filled one with shame for one's profession, it would have been amusing to listen to some of the comedies nightly played behind the scenes.

'Look here,' says the ghost of Hamlet's father, suddenly darting out of its dressing-room, and confronting the acting manager, who, thinking the coast was clear, has made a dash down the passage; 'look here, if I don't have something, I don't go on.'

'My dear boy,' replies the acting manager, in a tone of suppressed exasperation mingled with assumed sympathy, and glancing furtively about for a chance of escape, 'I really cannot. I have not got a penny. I will see you later on, when I shall have some money. I must go now. There is somebody waiting for me in front.'

'I don't care who is waiting for you in front. I've been waiting for you behind for two nights, and I mean to have some money.'

'How can I give you any money, when I haven't got any!' This is the gist of what he says. The embellishments had better not be added, here. Realism is an excellent thing in its way, but a Zola must draw the line somewhere.

After this, seeing that the actor looks determined, he begins to fumble in his pocket,

'I mean to have some money.'

and at last brings out half a crown, and presents it – without compliments.

'This won't do for me,' says the other, first pocketing the money; 'I can't live for four days on half a crown.'

Then the acting manager, with a further string of needless comments, thrusts five shillings into his hand, and rushes past, for he hears a footstep on the stairs, and fears another onslaught.

It is one of the chief characteristics of both managers and acting managers that they never do have any money. If caught holding it open in their hands, they always, from mere force of habit, say they haven't got any. A common answer to an appeal is: 'I really haven't got any money at all, my boy: how much do you want?'

The women, of course, could not bully for their money, but they shewed a quiet, never tiring persistence, more effective perhaps than all our storming. Certain it is that on the whole they were more successful than the men, and this might have been attributed to their sex's irresistible wheedling powers, if one could possibly have imagined such a thing as an acting manager open to humanizing influences.

Nobody grumbled at this state of things. The pleasure and surprise of getting any money at all was so great that the trouble of getting it was forgotten. They were too used to being robbed of all their earnings to mind being defrauded of only a part. An absconding manager was so common a thing that he did not even excite remark. He was regarded as something in the ordinary way of business, and his victims only sighed, when he was gone, and proceeded to look out for somebody else to cheat them.

And such another was by no means difficult to find in my time: the roll of theatrical managers teemed with thieves. It seemed to me that whenever a man got kicked out of everything else, he engaged as big a blackguard as himself for his acting manager and

The sex's irresistible wheedling powers

started a show. It must have been a profitable game, that played by these swindling managers, and there was no risk of any kind attending it. Nobody ever thought of interfering with them. If, by any clumsy accident on their own part, they did get within the clutches of the law, no harm came to them. County Court judges appeared to regard their frauds as mere practical jokes, and the worst they had to fear was a playful admonition of the 'Ah well, you mustn't do it again, you know,' kind.

In the profession itself, they were received with respect, as men of decided talent in their way. Even the most notorious of them were treated with civility, and care was taken never to mention before them such subjects as dishonesty and knavery, for fear of hurting their feelings. When actors and actresses went from London to Aberdeen to join Mr Smith's company, and found on arriving that Mr Smith was the same man

The Devonshire Park Theatre, Eastbourne, 1884: 1, The Auditorium; 2, Vestibule; 3, Exterior

who had already swindled them under half a dozen different names at half a dozen different times and places, what do you think they did? Shook hands cordially with the gentleman, made some pleasant observations about having met before, and hoped, in whispers among themselves, that he would not serve them the same this time! Of course, on the first Saturday night, while they were on the stage, he would run off with all the week's takings, go to the next town, and advertise for another company under the name of Jones.

It was no light matter for a man – and worse still for a poor girl – to be left without a penny or a friend in a strange town hundreds of miles from home. The poor players helped each other as well as they could, but provincial Pros. are – or, at least, were – not a wealthy class, and, after having paid their fares down, and kept themselves for a week or a fortnight, the most bloated capitalist among them rarely had more than a few shillings remaining in their pockets. Wardrobes had to be left as security with irate landladies, and, until they were redeemed or replaced, no other engagement was possible. Friends, poor enough themselves, goodness knows, had to be begged of. Every kind of valuable, even the wedding ring, had to be pawned, and the return home was made with troubled faces and empty hands.

The misery caused by these scoundrels makes one's blood boil to think of. I have known men and women forced to tramp home again half across the kingdom, seeking shelter in casual wards when the nights were too cold or wet to sleep under a haystack. I have known actors and actresses obliged to sell the clothes off their backs in order to get fresh stage wardrobes. I have known whole families, after having scraped together every penny they could get, so as to be able to join one of these companies, come back again a few days afterwards, utterly destitute, and compelled to sell the few sticks of furniture they had about the place before making another start. I knew one poor fellow, left penniless in Glasgow, with a delicate young wife near her confinement, and they had to come back to London by boat – steerage passage – for, after pledging everything, that was all they had money enough for. It was fearful weather in the middle of January, and the vessel tossed about in the Channel for over a week, and landed them just in time for the woman to die at home.

Some managers saved themselves the trouble of running away, and attempted to throw an air of respectability over the proceedings, by paying their company about one-and-sixpence apiece on treasury day, stating that they were very sorry, but that the thing had been a failure; that the houses had been all paper, the expenses unusually heavy, or any other of the stock lies always on hand. And he would think to comfort them by telling them that he himself had lost money, as though that were an unanswerable reason for their losing all theirs!

As to these men losing money of their own, that was impossible. They had not any to lose. Whatever they lost was somebody else's; of that you may be sure. They were men without any capital whatever, and they made use of actors merely as cat's paws in a speculation where all the risks were with the company, and all the advantages with themselves.

The 'share' system was worse even than this. It meant, in plain language, that, if the undertaking failed, the actors shared the losses amongst them, and, if it succeeded, the manager pocketed the profits.

As a matter of fact, actors were then the least con-sidered, and the most imposed upon of any people connected with the stage. If, at that time, one of my friends had started as a theatrical manager, I might, with a view of saving him unneces-sary expense, have given him the following hints:-

'You must pay your bill-poster, or he won't stick up your bills, or, if he does, it will be topsy-turvy. Pay for

your advertisements, or they won't get inserted. Pay your carpenters and scene-shifters, or they'll make it decidedly uncomfortable for you. Pay your money-takers, or they'll pay themselves; your gas, or it will be cut off; your rent, or you will be turned into the street. Be careful to pay the supers, too, or you'll find when it is time for them to go on that they've all gone off. For goodness sake, don't keep your charwoman waiting for her wages; you'll not have five minutes' quiet until she is satisfied. And if you don't wish to find yourself in the County Court on Monday morning, pay your call boy on Saturday night. You *must* pay these people. It is not a case of choice, there is simply no help for you; if you don't, you'll have to shut up shop in a couple of days. *But you needn't pay any one else.* If you have a few shillings left that you really don't know what to do with, you might divide it among the actors and actresses; but you can please yourself entirely about this. They work just the same whether they are paid or not.

'Your author, by the bye, is another person you never need pay. Indeed, in his case, it would be positively dangerous to do so. There is no telling what effect such a shock might have upon him.

'Your company will, it is true, pester you a good deal for their money, and grumble and threaten, but it never comes to anything, and, after a while, you get used to it, and don't mind.'

As to actors and actresses taking any actual measures for their own protection, the idea never occurred to them in their wildest dreams. If you suggested such a thing to them, it took their breath away, and you were looked upon as a young man with dangerous revolutionary tendencies that would some day get you into trouble. It was useless for one man to attempt to do anything by himself. I remember an actor summoning a manager who had cheated him out of seven pounds, and, after spending about ten pounds in costs, he got an order for payment by monthly instalments of ten shillings, not one of which, of course, he ever saw. After that, it was next to impossible for him to get a shop (this expression is not slang, it is a bit of local colour). No manager who had heard of the affair would engage him.

'A pretty pass the stage will come to,' said they, 'if this sort of thing is to become common.'

And the newspapers observed, it was a pity that he (the actor) should wash his dirty linen in public.

I have been careful to use the past tense all through these remarks. Some of them would apply very well to the present time, but, on the whole, things have improved since I was on the stage. I am glad of it.

CHAPTER 10

I Buy a Basket, and go into the Provinces

UR SEASON AT the London theatre came to a close early in December, and, about the end of November, we all began to take a great interest in the last page but one of 'The Actor's Bible'. Being just before Christmas, which is the busiest period of the theatrical year, there was no difficulty in getting another shop, for 'Useful people', 'Clever people', 'Talented people', 'Knockabout people', 'First-class High Kickers', 'Entire Dramatic Companies', were wanted here, there, and everywhere. I only answered one advertisement, and was engaged at once; but this, no doubt, was owing to my having taken the precaution, when applying, of enclosing my photograph.

I was to join the company a week before Christmas, at a town in the west of

England, where we were to open with pantomime. I was to give the first week for rehearsals at half salary, afterwards receiving a guinea a week for 'responsibles,' travelling expenses, when we went on tour, being paid by the management.

And here let me say that a more honourable and courteous gentleman than the manager of this company I never met. We did not even have to ask for our money; we were paid regularly, and to the last farthing, no matter whether business was good or bad. In short, he was an honest man, and as such held a conspicuous position among the theatrical managers of that day.

Previous to leaving London, I got together a small wardrobe. I already had a stock of boots and shoes, and tights, but these were only a few of the things required, and I found it rather an expensive matter before I had done. Varying in price from seven shillings to two pounds, wigs cost the most of anything, and I had to buy seven or eight of these – a 'white Court', a 'brown George', a 'flowing ringlets', a 'scratch' (why called a scratch I haven't the faintest notion), a 'comic old man', a 'bald', and a 'flow' for everything that one was not quite sure about.

I picked up a good many odds and ends of costume in Petticoat Lane one Sunday morning. It is a famous place for theatrical wardrobes. I got a complete sailor's suit for five shillings, and a suit of livery for sixteen. Old-fashioned swallow-tails and embroidered waistcoats, knee breeches, blouses, pants, hats, cloaks, and swords were also to be had there in plenty, and at very small cost. My sisters made me some more things (they had become reconciled to my 'mad trick' by this time, and had even got to rather like the idea of having an actor in the family), and for the rest I had to go to a regular costumier's. All these articles, together with a pretty complete modern wardrobe, a bundle of acting editions and other books, a 'make-up' box, a dressing-case, writing-case, etc., etc., made a pretty big pile, and, as this pile would be increased rather than diminished as time when on, I determined to get one big travelling basket to hold everything, and have done with it.

I did get a big one. I've got it now. It's down stairs in the washhouse. I've never been able to get rid of it from that day to this. I've tried leaving it behind when removing into new lodgings, but it has always been sent on after me, generally in a waggon with a couple of men, who, evidently imagining they were restoring me a treasured heirloom, have been disappointed at my complete absence of enthusiasm. I have lured stray boys into the house, and offered them half a crown to take it away and lose it, but they have become frightened, and gone home and told their mothers, and, after that it has got about in the neighbourhood that I have committed a murder. It isn't the sort of thing you can take out with you on a dark night, and drop down somebody else's area.

When I used it, I had to do all my packing in the hall, for it was impossible to get the thing up and down stairs. It always stood just behind the front door, which left about six inches of space for people to squeeze past, and every one that came in got more or less injured. The owner of the house, returning home late at night, would pitch head foremost over it, and begin yelling murder and police, under the impression it was burglars. The girl, coming in with the beer, would bang up against it, and upset the jug over it, when the whole contents would become saturated, and smell like a public-house.

The language used in connection with that basket was simply appalling. It roused railway porters and cabmen to madness, and the savage way in which they rushed upon it used to make my blood run cold. Landladies, who upon my first call had welcomed me with effusion, grew cool and distant when the basket arrived. Nobody had a good word for it. Everywhere it was hated and despised. I even feared that some day its victims would rise up and sweep it from the face of the earth. But no, it has survived both curses and kicks, and feeling it is hopeless ever to expect to get rid of it, I have made up my mind to be buried in it.

Faithful old basket! it is a good many years since you and I started on our travels that snowy seventeenth of December, and what a row we had with the cabman, ah me! But why did you desert me at Bristol? Why did you ——

But stay, wherefore should I go on apostrophizing the miserable old thing in this imbecile manner. And now I come to think of it, why too should I sit here sucking the end of my pen and scrowling savagely at the lamp, in the agonies of composition, when 'copy,' which one of The Leadenhall Press devils is plaguing me for (I do wish they'd send a boy who couldn't whistle), is lying ready to my hand?

Before me, borrowed for reference in penning these reminiscences, is a pile of letters, written during my travels to my old pal, Jim. Here's one:

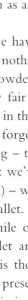

'Dear Jim, – We (the basket and I) had a terribly cold journey down. Lost the basket at Bristol and had to telegraph after it. That basket will be the death of me, I know. There is one advantage, though; it stamps you as an actor at once, and the porters don't expect any gratuities. Got jolly lodgings here. Nice, big bedroom, use of sitting-room, full attendance, and cooking for four bob a week. Pleasant, homely people, everything as clean as a new pin, and daughter rather pretty.

'I should have written before, but we have been so busy. Two and sometimes three rehearsals a day, to say nothing of painting the scenery, at which we all assisted. We had a crowded house for the opening on Boxing night, and have had very fair ones ever since – all over fifteen pounds. Serjeant Parry was in the stalls the other night, and a big London actor, whose name I forget just now. We (I say "we" because we all help in everything – two of us went out early a morning or two ago bill posting: we've got a regular bill poster, but it's his week for being drunk) – we, then, had a good deal of trouble training the supers and ballet. You should hear the supers dance: you can do so easily a mile off. They shake the whole building. Both they and the ballet are drawn from the fishing population of the town, and this is their first appearance on any stage. The ballet consists of eight at present, but that is only for the first go off, we shall reduce it to six in a little while. We have also

A provincial theatre

got about a dozen children to do a May-pole dance. It's a treat to see them. They are paid threepence a night, but they get three shillings' worth of enjoyment out of it for themselves. There is one little girl with the face of an angel – I honestly confess I've never seen an angel's face, and don't suppose I ever shall till I die, but I think it is that sort of face. She is dressed by seven every evening, and, from then, till she goes on the stage at ten, she is dancing and singing on her own account all over the place. When the May-pole is at last set up, she stands and gazes at it open-mouthed, and laughs to herself with glee. In her excitement, she always dances round the wrong way, and with the wrong boy – but it's always the same wrong boy, that is what makes it extraordinary. Happy wrong boy, only he doesn't know he's happy; he is so small. After the dance, the little boys kiss the little girls. You ought to see this little fairy turn aside and giggle, and push her little lover away. The boys are awfully shy over the business, but the little girls don't seem a bit afraid. Such is the superiority of women over man!

'The pantomime dresses all come from London, and are quite handsome and costly. The piece is *Whittington and his Cat*, written by the stage manager here, but it is nearly all songs and dances, and what little is spoken is more gag than book. I've two songs in one of my parts, and one in the other. I suppose singing is easy enough when you are used to it. It is the orchestra that puts me out, though. I should feel much freer without the music. We give them plenty of topical allusions on burning local questions, being careful, of course, to follow Mr Pickwick's advice, and "shout with the crowd." It fetches them immensely. The enthusiasm created nightly by a reference to the new lamp-post in the High-street is tremendous.

'Our low comedian is teaching me dancing, and I practise for about an hour a day. It's terribly hard work, but I can nearly do a hornpipe already. I want to do that: there is nothing knocks a country audience like a hornpipe.

'The stage manager is a surly fellow, of course; but the manager himself is a brick, and treats us – the actors – with as much respect as if we were stage carpenters; and money is safe. Our leading man has never turned up, so his part has been cut out, and this has not improved the plot. I play a lazy clerk in the opening (it's like going back to the old Civil Service days), and also prime minister of Tit-tattoo; having only three minutes for change. I get some legitimate fun out of the prime minister, but the clerk does not require artistic acting. I pretend to go to sleep, and then the clown, who plays another clerk, catches me over the head with a clapper, and then I wake up and catch him over the head with the clapper, and then he rushes at me and hits me, and I take the nap from him, and then he takes a nap from me (it wakes you up, this sort of nap, I tell you), after which we both have a grand struggle with the cat. I fell on my head the other night (lucky it wasn't any other part of me) and broke a chair in the course of this struggle. I got an encore for that, but didn't take it. I suppose you might call this knock-about business. I'm glad there are none of my friends here to see me. Acting isn't all making love in tights, and fighting with a real sword.

'We play a drama before the Panto. on Saturday next. Fancy me as the heavy father, blessing the stage manager and the leading lady, whose united ages amount to about eighty. That is what I'm going to do.

'We all dined with the manager on Christmas

'I have been recognised in the street, and followed by a small crowd of children.'

Day at his hotel, and had a very pleasant evening, keeping it up till four. We are each of us to have a 'ben.' before leaving here. I was rather pleased at this when I heard it, but the others displayed no rapture. Our walking gent. told me he never lost less than thirty shillings at his benefits. I don't think I shall take one. You pay all expenses, and have half the receipts. The attraction about it to my mind, though, is that you can put up what you like, and choose your own parts. I should like to have a try at Romeo.

'I have tasted fame and don't like it. I have been recognized in the street, and followed by a small crowd of children. They evidently expected me to stop at some corner and sing.

'The men's dressing-room at the theatre is up in the flies, and the only means of communication with

it is by a ladder. This got removed the other night, so that our low comedian couldn't get down. We didn't know this, however, so the Lord Chamberlain went on and said, "Behold your Prince approaches," and of course he didn't come. So the Lord Chamberlain said it again, and the house began to laugh; and then an excited voice from above cried out, "Shut up, you fool. Where's the ladder?"

'Must "shut up" myself now, for it's half-past seven, and I'm on at eight. I'm very comfortable down here. Write soon, old chap, and give us all the news. Have you seen dear little ——?'

Oh! the rest has nothing to do with theatrical matters.

In the wings – the first bouquet

CHAPTER 11

First Provincial Experience

THOUGHT I was safe for the summer with this company and congratulated myself on having found such good quarters. The glorious uncertainty of the boards, however, almost rivals that of the turf. From one reason and another, we broke up without ever going on tour, so that, two months after leaving London, I found myself back there on my way to the opposite side of the kingdom to join another company.

But, short as was my first country engagement, it gave me a pretty good insight into what provincial work was like. The following is from one of my letters, written after about a fortnight's experience of this work, which did not begin until the pantomime was withdrawn:

'The panto. is over. I wasn't by any means fond of it, but I'm sorry for one thing. While it was running, you see, there was no study or rehearsal, and we had the whole day free, and could – and did – enjoy ourselves. But no skating parties now! no long walks! no drives! no getting through a novel in one day! We play at least two fresh pieces every night and sometimes three. Most of them here already know their parts as well as they know their alphabet, but everything is new to me, and it is an awful grind. I can never tell until one night what I'm going to play the next. The cast is stuck up by the stage door every evening, and then, unless you happen to have the book yourself, you must borrow the stage manager's copy, and write out your part. If somebody else wants it, too, and is before you, you don't get hold of it till the next morning perhaps, and that gives you about eight hours in which to work up a part of say six or seven lengths (a "length" is forty-two lines).

'Sometimes there's a row over the cast. Second Low Comedy isn't going to play old men. That's not his line: he was not engaged to play old men. He'll see everybody somethinged first. – First Old Man wants to know what they mean by expecting him to play second old man's part. He has never been so insulted in his life. He has played with Keen and Macready and Phelps and Matthews, and they would none of them have dreamt of asking him to do such a thing. – Juvenile Lead has seen some rum things, but he is blowed if ever he saw the light comedy part given to the Walking Gentleman before. Anyhow, he shall decline to play the part given him, it's mere utility. – Walking Gent. says, well it really isn't his fault; he doesn't care one way or the other. He was cast for the part, and took it. – Juvenile Lead knows it isn't his fault – doesn't blame him at all – its the stage manager he blames. Juvenile Lead's opinion is that the stage manager is a fool. Everybody agrees with him here; it is our rallying point.

'The general result, when this sort of thing occurs, is that the part in dispute, no matter what it is, gets pitched on to me as "Responsibles". There's a little too much responsibility about my line. I like the way they put it, too, when they want me to take a particularly heavy part. They call it "giving me an opportunity!" If they mean an opportunity to stop up all night, I agree with them. That is the only opportunity I see about it. Do they suppose you are going to come out with an original and scholarly conception of the character, when you see the part for the first time the night before you play it? Why, you haven't time to think of the meaning of the words you repeat. But even if you had the chance of studying a character, it would be no use. They won't let you carry out your own ideas. There seems to be a regular set of rules for each part, and you are bound to follow them. Originality is at a discount in the provinces.

· ON THE STAGE – AND OFF ·

'I have lived to see our stage manager snubbed – sat upon – crushed. He has been carrying on down here, and swelling around to that extent you'd have thought him a station-master at the very least. Now he's like a bladder with the air let out. His wife's come.

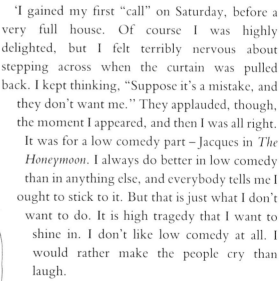

'The company is really getting quite familified. There are three married couples in it now. Our Low Comedian's wife is the Singing Chambermaid – an awfully pretty little woman (why have ugly men always got pretty wives?). I played her lover the other night, and we had to kiss two or three times. I rather liked it, especially as she doesn't make-up much. It isn't at all pleasant, getting a mouthful of powder or carmine.

'I gained my first "call" on Saturday, before a very full house. Of course I was highly delighted, but I felt terribly nervous about stepping across when the curtain was pulled back. I kept thinking, "Suppose it's a mistake, and they don't want me." They applauded, though, the moment I appeared, and then I was all right. It was for a low comedy part – Jacques in *The Honeymoon*. I always do better in low comedy than in anything else, and everybody tells me I ought to stick to it. But that is just what I don't want to do. It is high tragedy that I want to shine in. I don't like low comedy at all. I would rather make the people cry than laugh.

'There is one little difficulty that I have to contend with at present in playing comedy, and that is a tendency to laugh myself when I

'A calm sea' simulated by stagehands concealed under a 'sea cloth'

hear the house laughing. I suppose I shall get over this in time, but now, if I succeed in being at all comical, it tickles me as much as it does the audience, and, although I could keep grave enough if they didn't laugh, the moment they start I want to join in. But it is not only at my own doings that I am inclined to laugh. Anything funny on the stage amuses me, and being mixed up in it makes no difference. I played Frank to our Low Comedian's Major de Boots the other night. He was in extra good form and very droll, and I could hardly go on with my part for laughing at him. Of course, when a piece is played often, one soon ceases to be amused; but here, where each production enjoys a run of one consecutive night only, the joke does not pall.

'There is a man in the town who has been to the theatre regularly every night since we opened. The pantomime ran a month, and he came all through that. I know I was sick enough of the thing before it was over, but what I should have been, sitting it out from beginning to end every evening, I do not like to think. Most of our patrons, though, are pretty regular customers. The theatre-going population of the town is small but determined. Well, you see, ours is the only amusement going. There was a fat woman came last week, but she did not stay long. The people here are all so fat themselves they thought nothing of her.'

CHAPTER 12

'Mad Mat' takes advantage of an Opportunity

I HAD A day in London before starting off on my next venture, and so looked in at my old theatre. I knew none of the company, but the workmen and supers were mostly the same that I had left there. Dear old Jim was in his usual state, and greeted me with a pleasant –

'Hulloa! you seem jolly fond of the place *you* do. What the deuce brings *you* here?'

I explained that it was a hankering to see him once again.

'Mad Mat' was there, too. The pantomime was still running, and Mat played a demon with a pasteboard head. He was suffering great injustice nightly, so it appeared from what he told me. He was recalled regularly at the end of the scene in which he and his brother demons were knocked about by the low comedian, but the management would not allow him to go on again and bow.

'They are jealous,' whispered Mat to me, as we strolled into *The Rodney* (it would be unprofessional for an actor to meet a human creature whose swallowing organization was intact, and not propose a drink) – 'jealous, that's what it is. I'm getting too popular, and they think I shall cut them out.'

The poor fellow was madder than ever, and I was just thinking so at the very moment that he turned to me and said:

'Do you think I'm mad? candidly now.'

It's a little awkward when a maniac asks you point-blank if you think he's mad. Before I could collect myself sufficiently to reply, he continued:

'People often say I'm mad – *I've* heard them. Even if I am, it isn't the thing to throw in a gentleman's teeth, but I'm not – I'm not. *You* don't think I am, do you?'

I was that 'took aback,' as Mrs Brown would put it, that, if I had not had the presence of mind to gulp down a good mouthful of whisky and water, I don't know what I should have done. I then managed to get out something about 'a few slight eccentricities, per-haps, but——'

'That's it,' he cried excitedly, "eccentricities" – and they call that being mad. But they won't call me mad long – wait till I've made my name. They won't call me mad then. Mad! It's *they're* the fools, to think a man's mad when he isn't. Ha, ha, my boy, I'll surprise 'em one day. I'll shew the fools – the dolts – the idiots, who's been mad. "Great genius is to madness close allied." Who said that, eh? *He* was a genius, and they call *him* mad, perhaps. They're fools – all fools, I tell you. They can't tell the difference between madness and genius, but I'll shew them some day – some day.'

Fortunately there was nobody else in the bar where we were, or his ravings would have attracted an unpleasant amount of attention. He wanted to give me a taste of his quality then and there in his favourite *rôle* of Romeo, and I only kept him quiet by promising to call that night and hear him rehearse the part.

When we were ready to go out, I put my hand in my pocket to pay, but, to my horror, Mat was before me, and laid down the money on the counter. Nor would any argument induce him to take it up again. He was hurt at the suggestion even, and reminded me that I had stood treat on the last occasion – about three months ago. It was impossible to force the money on him. He was as proud on his six shillings a week as Croesus on sixty thousand a year, and I was compelled to let him have his way. So he paid the eightpence, and then we parted on the understanding that I was to see him later on at his 'lodgings.' – 'They are not what I could wish,' he explained, 'but you will, I am sure, overlook a few bachelor inconveniences. The place suits me well enough – for the present.'

Hearing a lunatic go through Romeo is not the pleasantest way of passing the night, but I should not have had pluck enough to disappoint the poor fellow, even if I had not

The Empire Music Hall, Newcastle, 1891

promised, and, accordingly, after having spent the evening enjoying the unusual luxury of sitting quiet, and seeing other people excite them-selves for *my* amusement, I made my way to the address Mat had given me.

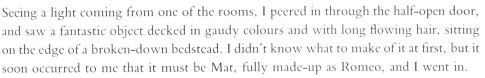

The house was in a narrow court at the back of the New Cut. The front door stood wide open, though it was twelve o'clock, and a bitterly cold night. A child lay huddled up on the doorstep, and a woman was sleeping in the passage. I stumbled over the woman, groping my way along in the dark. She seemed used to being trodden upon though, for she only looked up unconcernedly, and went to sleep again at once. Mat had told me his place was at the very top, so I went on until there were no more stairs, and then I looked round me.

Seeing a light coming from one of the rooms, I peered in through the half-open door, and saw a fantastic object decked in gaudy colours and with long flowing hair, sitting on the edge of a broken-down bedstead. I didn't know what to make of it at first, but it soon occurred to me that it must be Mat, fully made-up as Romeo, and I went in.

I thought, when I had seen him a few hours before, that he looked queer – even for him – but now, his haggard face daubed with paint, and his great eyes staring out of it more wildly than ever, he positively frightened me. He held out his hand, which was thin and white, but remained seated.

'Excuse my rising,' he said slowly, in a weak voice, 'I feel so strange. I don't think I can go through the part to-night. So sorry to have brought you here for nothing, but you must come and see me some other time.'

I got him to lie down on the bed just as he was, and covered him with the old rags that were on it. He lay still for a few minutes, then he looked up and said:

'I won't forget you, L——, when I'm well off. You've been friendly to me when I was poor: I shan't forget it, my boy. My opportunity will soon come now – very soon, and then——'

He didn't finish the sentence, but began to murmur bits of the part to himself, and in a little while he dropped asleep. I stole softly out, and went in search of a doctor. I got hold of one at last, and returned with him to Mat's attic. He was still asleep, and after arranging matters as well as I could with the doctor, I left, for I had to be on my way early in the morning.

I never expected to see Mat again, and I never did. People who have lived for any length of time on six shillings a week don't take long to die when they set about it, and, two days after I had seen him, Mad Mat's opportunity came, and he took it.

CHAPTER 13.

Lodgings and Landladies

T HEY CHARGED ME extra for the basket on the Great Eastern Line, and I have hated that company ever since. Of course it was over weight, but actors are good customers to the railways, and a little excess luggage is not, as a rule, too closely inquired into. The myrmidons at Bishopsgate, however, were inexorable. It was in vain I tried to persuade them that the thing was 'as light as a feather.' They insisted on sticking it up edgeways on a shaky iron plate, and wobbling something up and down a bar; afterwards giving me an absurd bit of paper with '4*s.* 4*d.*' on it, which, I explained, I didn't want, but which they charged me for just as though I had specially ordered it.

My destination was a small market town in the eastern counties, where I arrived about mid-day. It was the most dead and alive place I have ever been to. All eastern

Act 1st

"Colleen Bawn" transparent Mountain cloth
Water row x — thickness stone wall x 14th Cut
Ship with rostrum L. Whittington felucca
shop pieces R & L. Watsons new blue tent
piece, set L.H — Wood wings & borders

Act 2nd

Corinthian palace Screen cloth — — 1th
Garden cloth   5th
Platform steps and balustrades

Act 3

1st Watson new cut cave cloth — 1
Rostrum and narrow steps behind it LH
Gordons transparent mountain cloth 2nd
Rock ground row x
Gauze descends at cue
Alice in Wonderland "scrim cloth descends
behind gauze at cue. Stone cross on bridge
Transparent cloth
                                    ground row
___ [L] Bridge   ▓STEPS▓ ‖ Rostrum ___
cut   cut
cloth   cloth

See lithograph next page

Set instructions for the Prince's Theatre, Bristol, 1887 for a production of *Robert the Devil* by Meyerbeer

county towns are more or less dead and alive – particularly the former – but this one was dreariness personified. Not a soul was to be seen outside the station. In the yard stood a solitary cab to which was attached a limp horse that, with head hanging down and knees bent out, looked the picture of resigned misery; but the driver had disappeared – washed away by the rain, perhaps, which was pouring steadily down. I left my belongings in the cloak room and walked straight to the theatre. I passed two or three green posters on my way, headed 'Theatre Royal', and setting forth that '——, the World-Renowned Tragedian from Drury Lane,' would give his magnificent impersonations from *Richard III* and *The Idiot Witness* that night, and begging the inhabitants, for their own sakes, to 'come early'. I found the whole company assembled on the stage, and looking as dismal as the town itself. They all had colds in the head, including the manager, 'the World-Renowned Tragedian from Drury Lane', who had the face-ache into the bargain.

After a rough and ready rehearsal of the tragedy, melodrama, and burlesque to be played that evening (I had had all my parts sent me by post before joining), I started off by myself to look for lodgings, as I had come to the conclusion that my own society would, on the whole, be less depressing than that of any gentleman in the company.

Lodging hunting is by no means the most pleasant business connected with touring. It always means an hour or two's wandering up and down back streets, squinting up at windows, knocking at doors, and waiting about on doorsteps. You are under the impression all the while that the entire street is watching you and that it has put you down as either a begging letter impostor, or else as the water-rate man, and despises you accordingly. You never find the place that suits you until you have been everywhere else. If you could only begin at the end and work backwards, the search would be over at once. But, somehow or other, you can never manage to do this, and you have always to go through the same routine. First of all, there are the places that ask about twice as much as you are prepared to give, and at which you promise to call again when you have seen your friend. Then there are the places that are just taken, or just going to be taken, or just not to be taken. There are places where you can have half a bed with another gentleman, the other gentleman generally being the billiard-marker at the hotel opposite, or some journeyman photographer. There are the people who won't take you because you are not a married couple, and the people who won't take you because you are a play-actor, and the people who want you to be out all day, and the people who want you to be in by ten. Added to these, there is the slatternly woman, who comes to the door, followed by a mob of dirty children, that cling to her skirts and regard you with silent horror, evidently thinking that the 'big ugly man', so often threatened, has really come this time. Or the fool of a husband, who scratches his head and says you had better call again, when the 'missus' is in. Or, most aggravating of all, the woman who stands on the step, after you have gone, and watches you down the street, so that you don't like to knock anywhere else.

All this I was prepared for when I started, but no such ordeal was in store for me. The difficulty of selecting lodgings was got rid of altogether in the present case by there simply being no lodgings of any kind to be let. It had evidently never occurred to the inhabitants of this delightful spot that any human being could possibly desire to lodge there, and I don't wonder at it. There were a couple of inns in the High Street, but country actors cannot afford inns however moderate, and of 'Furnished Apartments' or 'Bed Rooms for Single Gentlemen' there were none. I explored every street in the town without coming across a single bill, and then, as a last resource, I went into a baker's shop to inquire. I don't know why bakers should be better acquainted than any other tradesmen with the private affairs of their neighbours, but that they are has always been my impression, or, at least, *had* been up till then, when it received a rude blow. I asked two bakers, and both of them shook their heads, and knew of no one who let lodgings. I was in despair, and the High Street, when I glanced up and saw a very pleasant face smiling at me from the door of a milliner's shop. Somehow, the sight of it inspired me with hope. I smiled back, and ——

'Could the owner of the pleasant face recommend me to any lodgings?'

The painter's studio, Haymarket Theatre, London, 1873

'Was Monsieur going to stop in the town?'

The owner of the pleasant face looked surprised. 'Was Monsieur going to stop in the town?'

On Monsieur explaining that he was an actor, Madame was delighted, and smiled more pleasantly than ever. 'Madame did so love the theatre. Had not been to one for, oh! so long time; not since she did leave Regent Street – the Regent Street that was in our London. Did Monsieur know London? Had been to heaps and heaps of theatres then. And at Paris. Ah, Paris! Ah, the theatres at Paris! Ah! But there was nothing to go to here. It was so quiet, so stupid, this town. We English, we did seem so dull. Monsieur, son mari, he did not mind it. He had been born here. He did love the sleepiness – the what we did call the monotony. But Madame, she did love the gaiety. This place was, oh, so sad.'

Here Madame clasped her hands – pretty little hands they were, too – and looked so piteous, that Monsieur felt strongly inclined to take her in his arms and comfort her. He, however, on second thoughts, restrained his generous impulse.

Madame then stated her intention to go to the theatre that very evening, and requested to know what was to be played.

On Monsieur informing her that '——, the World-Renowned Tragedian from Drury Lane, would give his magnificent impersonations of *Richard III* and *The Idiot Witness*,' she seemed greatly impressed, and hoped it was a comedy. Madame loved comedies. 'To laugh at all the fun – to be made merry – that was so good.'

Monsieur thought that Madame would have plenty to laugh at in the magnificent impersonations of *Richard III* and *The Idiot Witness*, even if she found the burlesque a little heavy, but he didn't say so.

Then Madame remembered Monsieur was looking for lodgings. Madame put the top of her forefinger in her mouth, puckered her brows, and looked serious. 'Yes, there was Miss Kemp, she had sometimes taken a lodger. But Miss Kemp was so strict, so particular. She did want every one to be so good. Was Monsieur good?' This with a doubting smile.

Monsieur hazarded the opinion that having gazed into Madame's eyes for five minutes was enough to make a saint of any man. Monsieur's opinion was laughed at, but, nevertheless notwithstanding, Miss Kemp's address was given him, and thither he repaired, armed with the recommendation of his charming little French friend.

Miss Kemp was an old maid, and lived by herself in a small three-cornered house that stood in a grass-grown courtyard behind the church. She was a prim old lady, with quick eyes and a sharp chin. She looked me up and down with two jerks of her head, and then supposed that I had come to the town to work.

'No,' I replied, 'I had come to play. I was an actor.'

'Oh,' said Miss Kemp. Then added severely, 'You're married.'

I repudiated the insinuation with scorn.

After that, the old lady asked me inside, and we soon became friends. I can always get on with old ladies. Next to young ones, I like them better than any other class of the community. And Miss Kemp was a very nice old lady. She was as motherly as a barnyard hen, though she was an old maid. I suggested going out again to buy a chop for my tea, and to fetch my basket, but she wouldn't hear of it.

'Bless the child,' said she, 'do run and take off those wet boots. I'll send some one for your luggage.'

So I was made to take off my coat and boots, and to sit by the fire, with my feet wrapped up in a shawl, while Miss Kemp bustled about with toast and steaks, and rattled the tea-things and chatted.

I only stopped a week with Miss Kemp, that being the length of time the company remained in the town, but it will be a long while before I forget the odd little old maid with her fussy ways and kindly heart. I can still see, in memory, the neat kitchen with its cheerful fire in polished grate, before which sleek purring Tom lies stretched. The

old-fashioned lamp burns brightly on the table, and, between it and the fire, sits the little old lady herself in her high-backed chair, her knitting in her hands and her open Bible on her knee. As I recall the picture, so may it still be now, and so may it still remain for many a year to come.

I must have been singularly fortunate in regard to landladies, or else they are a very much maligned class. I have had a good deal to do with them, and, on the whole, I have found them kind, obliging and the very reverse of extortionate. With country land-ladies, especially. I have ever been most comfortable, and even among London ones, who, as a class, are not so pleasant as their provincial sisters, I have never, as yet, come across a single specimen of that terrible she-dragon about which I have heard so much. To champion the cause of landladies is rather an extraordinary proceeding, but, as so much is said against them, I think it only fair to state my own experience. They have their faults. They bully the slavey (but then the slavey sauces them, so per-

haps it is only tit for tat), they will fry chops, and they talk enough for an Irish M.P. They persist in telling you all their troubles, and they keep you waiting for your breakfast while they do it. They never tire of recounting to you all they have done for some ungrateful relative, and they bring down a drawer-ful of letters on the subject, which they would like you to cast your eye through. They bore you to death every day, too, with a complete record of the sayings and doings of some immaculate young man lodger they once had. This young man appears to have been quite over-weighted with a crushing sense of the goodness of the landlady in question. Many and many a time has he said to her, with tears in his eyes: 'Ah, Mrs So-and-so, you have been more than a mother to me;' and then he has pressed her hand, and felt he could never repay her kindness. Which seems to have been the fact, for he has generally gone off, in the end, owing a pretty considerable sum.

Rehearsing for the pantomime, 1887

CHAPTER 14

With a Stock Company

IT WAS MOST miserable with the company I had now joined. What it was like may be gathered from the following:

'Dear Jim, – If I stop long with this company I shall go mad (not very far to go perhaps you'll say!). I must get out of it soon. It's the most wretched affair you could possibly imagine. Crummles's show was a *Comédie Française* in its arrangements compared with this. We have neither stage-manager nor acting-manager. If this were all, I shouldn't grumble; but we have to do our own bill posting, help work the scenes, and take the money at the doors – not an arduous task, this last. There are no "lines". We are all "responsibles", and the parts are distributed among us with the utmost impartiality. In the matter of salary, too, there is the same charming equality: we all get a guinea. In theory, that is: in reality, our salaries vary according to our powers of nagging; the maximum ever attained by any one having been fifteen shillings. I wonder we get any, though, considering the audiences we play to. The mere sight of the house gives one the horrors every night. It is so dimly lighted (for, to save expense, the gas is only turned a quarter on) that you can hardly see your way about, and so empty, that every sound echoes and re-echoes through the place, till it seems as though a dozen people are talking in a scene where there are only two. You walk on the stage, and there in front of you are, say, twenty people dotted about the pit, a few more are lolling listlessly over the gallery rails, and there are two or three little groups in the boxes, while, as a background to these patches of unhappy humanity, there stares out the bare boards and the dingy upholstery. It is impossible to *act* among such surroundings as these. All you can do is to just drag through your part, and the audience, who one and all have evidently been regretting from the very first that they ever came – a fact they do not even attempt to disguise – are as glad when it is over as you are. We stop a week in each town and play the same pieces, so, of course, there is no study or rehearsal now. But I wish there were; anything would be better than this depressing monotony.

'I might have guessed what sort of a company it was by his sending me the parts he did. I play Duncan, Banquo, Seyton, and a murderer in *Macbeth*; Tybalt and the Apothecary in *Romeo and Juliet*; and Laertes, Osric, and the Second Player in *Hamlet* – and so on all through. None of us play less than two parts in the same piece. No sooner are we killed or otherwise disposed of as one person, than we are up again as somebody else, and that, almost before we have time to change our clothes. I sometimes have to come on as an entirely new party with no other change than the addition of a beard. It puts me in mind of the nigger who borrowed his master's hat with the idea of passing himself off as "one of them white folk". I should think that if the audience – when there are any – attempt to understand the play, they must have a lively time of it; and if they are at all acquainted with our National Bard, they must be still more puzzled. We have improved so on the originals, that the old gentleman himself would never recognize them. They are one-third Shakespeare, and two-thirds the Renowned Tragedian from Drury Lane.

'Of course, I have not had my railway fare, which I was promised after joining, and I've given up asking for it now. . .'.

I got a chance of changing my quarters after a few weeks, and I need scarcely say I jumped at it. We passed through a big town that was the head-quarters of an

On Wednesday Evening, April 4th,

Will be presented the Melo-Dramatic Play called

TWM
Shon Catty,

OR THE

WELSH
ROB ROY.

Written by J. Moncrieff, Esq. Author of "Where shall we dine," " Spectre Bridegroom," &c.
As performed in London with Universal Applause.

WELSH

Twm Shon Catty (the Welsh Rob Roy)........Mr. FITZWAYLETT

Madoc........Mr. ROE	Sir Owen Glendower........Mr. CLARKSON	
Taffy (Son of Ap Jenkins)........Mr. ROSS	Hoel (with a characteristic Song)........Mr. HENRY	
Mrs. Owen Ap Jenkins........Mrs. FREDERICK	And, Eleanor (the Lady of Landisent)........Miss PITT.	

ENGLISH IN ARMS AGAINST THE WELSH.

Henry, Earl of Percy, (surnamed Hotspur)....Mr. BRINDAL	Earl of Northumberland........Mr. HORSMAN
Mortimer (Earl of March)........Mr. HUGHES	Sir Hugh Vernon........Mr. SMITH

ENGLISH IN ARMS FOR THE KING.

Henry (Son of Henry IV. and Prince of Wales) Mr. GARTON	Sir John Falstaff........Mr. MATTHEWS
Roderick Arundel (Favourite of the Prince)....Mr. M'GILL	And, Corporal Pistol........Mr. DUFF

IN THE COURSE OF THE PIECE A GRAND BATTLE.

To which will be added the laughable Interlude called The

Village Lawyer,

Which was received on Wednesday Evening last with the most Rapturous Applause.

Scout........Mr. BAKER	Justice Mittimus........Mr. HORSMAN
Snarl........Mr. DUFF	Sheepface........Mr. ROSS
Charles........Mr. M'GILL	Constable........Mr. WESTON
Kate........Miss CARR	Mrs. Scout........Mrs. FREDERICK.

To conclude with the Musical Romance of

Blue Beard

OR, FEMALE CURIOSITY.

Written by Colman; the Music by Kelly.
With splendid New Scenery, Dresses, Banners, Processions, Decorations, &c. &c.

Abomilique (Blue Beard)........Mr. CLARKSON

Sellm........Mr. HENRY

Ibrahim........Mr. DUFF	Second Spahi........Mr. HUGHES
Shacabac........Mr. BAKER	Third Spahi........Mr. ALDRIDGE
Hassan........Mr. ROSS	Fourth Spahi........Mr. ROE
First Spahi........Mr. HORSMAN	Slave........Mr. WESTON
Fatima........Miss TAYLOR	Irene........Miss PITT	And, Beda......Mrs. BRINDAL.	

The Scenery and Machinery chiefly consist of

ABOMILIQUE'S PROCESSIONS,
PALANQUIN, ELEPHANT, CAMELS, &c. &c.
ILLUMINATED GARDEN,
BLUE CHAMBER, SEPULCHRE
IN WHICH ABOMILIQUE IS DESTROYED, &c.

By Eminent Artists, under the direction of Mr. DONALDSON.

THE DANCE, BY MISS LANCASTER & MISS WILKINS.

For the BENEFIT of Miss DILLON SULLIVAN.—On Thursday Evening will be presented The BEGGARS' OPERA. After which the favourite Drama, in one act, called THE SCAPE-GOAT. To conclude with, second time, a New Farce, called DRENCHED AND DRIED.

The Grand Historical Drama of KENILWORTH, or England's Golden Days, was received on Monday Evening with the most Rapturous Applause, by a Crowded and Overflowing House; it will be repeated on Friday Evening, when Mrs. M'CREADY's Outstanding Tickets will be admitted; being the Last Night of performing until the Easter Holidays.

Tickets, and Places in the Boxes, to be had at the Theatre, from Eleven till Three o'clock.
Tickets for the Pit and Gallery to be had at the General Printing-Office, 9. Narrow Wine-Street

SOMERTON, Printer.

established circuit company, and, hearing that one of their 'responsibles' had just left, I went straight to the manager, offered myself, and was accepted. Of course, in the usual way, I ought to have given a fortnight's notice to the other manager, but, under the circumstances, this could hardly have been insisted upon. So I made the Renowned Tragedian from Drury Lane a present of all the arrears of salary he owed me – at which generosity on my part we both grinned – and left him at once. I don't think he was very sorry. It saved him a few shillings weekly, for my place was filled by one of the orchestra, that body being thereby reduced to two.

The company of which I was now a member was one of the very few stock companies then remaining in the provinces. The touring system had fairly set in by this time, and had, as a consequence, driven out the old theatrical troupes that used to act on from year to year within the same narrow circle, and were looked upon as one of the institutions of the half-dozen towns they visited. I am not going to discuss here the rival merits or demerits of the two systems. There are advantages and disadvantages to be urged on both sides, not only from the 'school' point of view, but also as regards the personal interests and comfort of the actor. I will merely say, with reference to the latter part of the question, that I myself preferred the bustle and change of touring. Indeed, in spite of all the attending anxieties and troubles, it was in this constant change – this continual shifting of the panorama of scenes and circumstances by which I was

The orchestra reduced to two

surrounded – that, for me, the chief charm of stage life lay. Change of any kind is always delightful to youth; whether in big things or in little ones. We have not been sufficiently seasoned by disappointment in the past, then, to be sceptical as to all favours the Future may be holding for us in her hand. A young man looks upon every change as a fresh chance. Fancy paints a more glowing fortune for each new departure, and at every turn in the road he hopes to burst upon his goal.

At each new town I went to, and with each new company I joined, new opportunities for the display of my talents would arise. The genius that one public had ignored, another would recognize and honour. In minor matters, too, there was always pleasant expectation. Agreeable companions and warm friends might be awaiting me in a new company, the lady members might be extraordinarily lovely, and money might be surer. The mere travelling, the seeing strange towns and country, the playing in different theatres, the staying in different lodgings, the occasional passing through London and looking in at home, all added to the undoubted delight I felt in this sort of life, and fully reconciled me to its many annoyances.

But being fixed in a dull country town for about six months at a stretch, with no other recreation than a game of cards, or a gossip in an inn parlour, I didn't find at all pleasant. To the staid, or to the married members, I daresay it was satisfactory enough. They had, some of them, been born in the company, and had been married in the company, and they hoped to die in the company. They were known throughout the circuit. They took an interest in the towns, and the towns took an interest in them, and came to their benefits. They returned again and again to the same lodgings. There was no fear of their forgetting where they lived, as sometimes happened to a touring actor on the first day in a new town. They were not unknown vagabonds wandering houseless from place to place; they were citizens and townsmen, living among their friends and relations. Every stick of furniture in their rooms was familiar to them. Their lodgings were not mere furnished apartments, but 'home,' or as near to a home as a country player could ever expect to get. No doubt they, as Madame would have said, 'did love the sleepiness;' but I, an energetic young bachelor, found it 'oh! so sad.'

Sad as I might have thought it though, I stayed there five months, during which time I seem to have written an immense number of letters to the long-suffering Jim. All that is worth recording here, however, is contained in the following extracts:

'. . . The work is not so hard now. It was very stiff at first, as we changed the bill about every other night, but I got hold of the *répertoire* and studied up all the parts that I knew I should have to play. It still comes heavy when there is a benefit, especially when anything modern is put up, as, then, having a good wardrobe, I generally get cast for the "gentlemanly party", and that is always a lengthy part. But what makes it still more difficult, is the way everybody gags. Nobody speaks by the book here. They equivocate, and then I am undone.

I never know where I am. The other day, I had a particularly long part given me to play the next evening. I stayed up nearly all night over it. At rehearsal in the morning, the light-comedy, with whom I was principally concerned, asked me how I'd got on. "Well, I think I shall know something about it," I answered. "At all events, I've got the cues perfect." "Oh! don't bother yourself about cues," replied he, cheerfully. "You won't get a blessed cue from me. I use my own words now. Just you look out for the sense."

'I did look out for the sense, but I'll be hanged if I could see any in what he said. There was no doubt as to the words being his own. How I got through with it I don't know. He helped me with suggestions when I stuck, such as: "Go on, let off your bit about a father," or "Have you told me what Sarah said?"

'Get me a pair of second-hand tights at Stinchcombe's, will you, and have them washed and sent down. Any old things will do. I only want them to wear underneath others. I have to appear in black tights next Monday. They make your legs look so awfully thin, and I'm not too stout in those parts as it is.

'I have got hold of an invaluable pair of boots (well, so they ought to be, I paid fifteen shillings for them). Pulled up to their full height, they reach nearly to the waist, and are a pair of American jack-boots; doubled in round the calf, and with a bit of gold lace and a tassel pinned on, they are hessians; with painted tops instead of

The star trap used by a clown

the gold lace and tassel, they are hunting boots; and wrinkled down about the ankle, and stuck out round the top, they are either Charles or Cromwell, according to whether they are ornamented with lace and a bow, or left plain. You have to keep a sharp eye on them, though, for they have a habit of executing changes on their own account unbeknown to you, so that while one of your legs is swaggering about as a highwayman, the other is masquerading as a cavalier. We dress the pieces very well indeed here. There is an excellent wardrobe belonging to the theatre.

'I do wish it were possible to get the programmes made out by intelligent men, instead of by acting-managers. If they do ever happen, by some strange accident, not to place your name opposite the wrong character, they put you down for a part that never existed; and if they get the other things right, they spell your name wrong.

'I say, here's a jolly nice thing, you know; they've fined me half a crown for not attending rehearsal. Why, I was there all the while, only I was over the way, and when I came back they had finished. That's our fool of a prompter, that is; he knew where I was. I'll serve him out.'

· CHAPTER *15* ·

Revenge!

ORE EXTRACTS:

'. . . I'm afraid I shall have to trouble you to get me another wig. I thought my own hair would do for modern juvenile parts, but it isn't considered light enough. "Be virtuous and you will have hair the colour of tow," seems to be the basis of the whole theatrical religion. I wish I could be as economical in wigs as our First Old Man is. He makes one do for everything. He wears it the right way when he is a serious old man, and hind part foremost when he wants to be funny.

'Talking of wigs puts me in mind of an accident our manager had the other night. He is over fifty, but he fancies he is a sort of Charles Mathews, and will play young parts. So on Saturday evening he came on as the lover in an old English comedy, wearing one of those big three-cornered hats. "Who is that handsome young man with the fair hair?" says the heroine to her confidante. "Oh, that, why that is Sir Harry Monfort, the gallant young gentleman who saved the Prince's life. He is the youngest officer in the camp, but already the most famous." "Brave boy," murmurs the heroine; "I would speak a word with him. Call him hither, Leonora." So Leonora called him thither, and up he skipped. When the heroine spoke to him, he was quite overcome with boyish bashfulness. "Ah, madam," sighed he, taking off his hat and making a sweeping bow – "What the devil's the matter? What are they laughing at? Oh my ——"

'He had taken his wig off with his hat, and there was the "brave boy's" poor old bald head exposed to the jeers of a ribald house.

'I'd half a mind to rush up to town last week. I was out of the bill for three nights running. But the mere railway fare would have cost me nearly half a week's salary, so I contented myself with a trip over to R—— and a look in at the show there. I met W——. He's married little Polly——, who was walking lady at——. She is up at Aberdeen now, and he hasn't seen her for over three months. Rather rough on a young couple who haven't been married a year. The old ones bear up against this sort of thing very well indeed, but poor W—— is quite upset about it. They kept together as long as they could, but business got so bad that they had to separate, and each take the first thing that offered. . .'.

'You remember my telling you how our prompter got me fined for not attending a rehearsal some time ago. I said I would serve him out, and so I have. Or rather *we* have – I and one of the others who had a score against him – for he's a bumptious, interfering sort of fellow, and makes himself disagreeable to everybody. He is awful spoons on a Miss Pinkeen, whose father keeps an ironmonger's shop next door to the theatre. The old man knows nothing about it, and they are up to all kinds of dodges to get a word with each other. Now, one of our dressing-room windows is exactly opposite their staircase window, and he and the girl often talk across; and, once or twice, he has placed a plank between the two windows, and crawled along it into the house when her father has been away. Well, we got hold of a bit of this girl's writing the other day, and forged

'They are up to all kinds of dodges to get a word with each other.'

a letter to him, saying that her father had gone out, and that she wanted to see him very particularly, and that he was to come over through the window and wait on the landing till she came upstairs. Then, just before rehearsal, we went out and gave a stray boy twopence to take it in to him.

'Of course, no sooner did we see that he was fairly inside the house, and out of sight, than we pulled the board in and shut our window. It got quite exciting on the stage as time went by. "Where's ——?" fumed the stage manager. "Where the devil's——? It's too bad of him to keep us all waiting like this." And then the call boy was sent round to four public houses, and then to his lodgings; for he had got the book in his pocket, and we couldn't begin without him. "Oh, it's too bad of him to go away and stop like this," cried the stage manager again at the end of half an hour. "I'll fine him five shillings for this. I won't be played the fool with." In about an hour he came in looking thunder and lightning. He wouldn't give any explanation. All we could get out of him was, that if he could find out who'd done it, he'd jolly well wring his neck.

'From what the ironmonger's boy told our call-boy, it seems that he waited about three-quarters of an hour on the stairs, not daring to move, and that then the old man came up and wanted to know what he was doing there. There was a regular scene in the house, and the girl has sworn that she'll never speak to him again for getting her into a row, and about four of her biggest male relatives have each expressed a firm determination to break every bone in his body; and the boy adds, that from his knowledge of them they are to be relied upon. We have thought it our duty to let him know these things.'

I find nothing further of any theatrical interest, until I come to the following, written about four months after the date of my entering the company:

'I was far too busy to write last week. It's been something awful. We've got —★ down here for a fortnight. His list consists of eighteen pieces – eight "legitimate", five dramas, four comedies, and a farce; and we only had a week in which to prepare. There have been rehearsals at ten, and rehearsals at three, and rehearsals at eleven, after the performance was over. First, I took all the parts given me, and studied them straight off one after the other. Then I found I'd got them all jumbled up together in my head and the more I tried to remember what belonged to which, the more I forgot which belonged to what. At rehearsal I talked Shakespeare in the farce, and put most of the farce and a selection from all the five dramas into one of the comedies. And then the stage manager went to put me right, and then *he* got mixed up, and wanted to know if anybody could oblige him by informing him what really was being rehearsed; and the Leading Lady and the First Low Comedy said it was one of the dramas,

★ A 'Star' from London.

She is dead! You have poisoned her! – a scene from *The Balloon* by H.H. Darnley and G. Manville Fenn, Strand Theatre, February 1889

but the Second Low Comedy, the Soubrette, and the Leader of the orchestra would have it was a comedy, while the rest of us was too bewildered to be capable of forming any opinion on any subject.

'The strain has so upset me, that I don't even now know whether I'm standing on my head or my heels; and our First Old Man – but I'll come to him later on. My work has been particularly heavy, for, in consequence of a serious accident that has happened to our Walking Gentleman, I've had to take his place. He was playing a part in which somebody – the Heavy man – tries to stab him while he's asleep. But just when the would-be murderer has finished soliloquizing, and the blow is about to fall, he starts up, and a grand struggle ensues. I think the other fellow must have been drunk on the last occasion. Anyhow, the business was most clumsily managed, and R ——, our Walking Gent., got his eye cut out, and is disfigured for life. It is quite impossible for him now to play his old line, and he has to do heavies or low comedy, or anything where appearance is of no importance. The poor fellow is terribly cut up – don't think I'm trying to make a ghastly joke – and he seems to be especially bitter against me for having slipped into his shoes. I'm sure he need not be; whatever good his ill wind has blown me has brought with it more work than it's worth; and I think, on the whole, taking this star business into consideration, I would rather have stopped where I was. I knew a good many of the parts I should have had to play, but, as it is, everything has been fresh study.

'Well, I was going to tell you about our old man. He had always boasted that he hadn't studied for the last ten years. I don't know what particular merit there was in this, that he should have so prided himself upon it, but that he considered it as highly clever on his part there could not be the slightest doubt; and he had even got to quite despise anyone who did study. You can imagine his feelings, therefore, when sixteen long parts, eleven at least of which he had never seen before, were placed in his hand, with a request that he would be letter perfect in all by the following Thursday. It was observed that he didn't say much at the time. He was a garrulous old gentleman as a rule, but, after once glancing over the bundle, he grew thoughtful and abstracted, and did not join in the chorus of curses loud and deep which was being sung with great vigour by the rest of the company. The only person to whom he made any remark was myself, who happened to be standing by the stage-door when he was going out. He took the bundle of parts out of his pocket, and shewed them to me. "Nice little lot, that – ain't it?" he said. "I'll just go home and study them all up –

'He started, and uttered an exclamation of horror.'

that's what I'll do." Then he smiled – a sad, wan smile – and went slowly out.

'That was on Saturday evening, and on Monday morning we met at ten for rehearsal. We went on without the old man until eleven, and then, as he hadn't turned up, and was much wanted, the boy was despatched to his lodgings to see if he was there. We waited patiently for another quarter of an hour, and then the boy returned.

'The old man had not been seen since Sunday.

'His landlady had left him in the morning, looking over the "parts," and when she returned in the evening, he was gone. A letter, addressed to her, had been found in his room, and this she had given the boy to take back with him.

'The stage manager took it and hurriedly opened it. At the first glance, he started and uttered an exclamation of horror; and when he had finished it, it dropped from his hand, and he sank down in the nearest chair, dazed and bewildered, like a man who has heard, but cannot yet grasp, some terrible news.

'A cold, sickly feeling came over me. The strange, far-away look, and the quiet, sad smile that I had last seen on the old man's face came back to me with startling vividness, and with a new and awful meaning. He was old and enfeebled. He had not the elastic vigour of youth that can bear up under worry and work. His mind, to all seeming, had never at any time been very powerful. Had the sudden and heavy call upon its energies actually unhinged it? and had the poor old fellow in some mad moment taken up arms against his sea of troubles, and by opposing ended them? Was he now lying in some shady copse, with a gaping wound from ear to ear, or sleeping his last sleep with the deep waters for a coverlet? Was what lay before me a message from the grave? These thoughts flashed like lightning through my brain as I darted forward and picked the letter up. It ran as follows:

"Dear Mrs Hopsam, – I'm off to London by the 3.30, and shan't come back. I'll write and let you know where to send my things. I left a pair of boots at Jupp's to have the toe-caps sewn – please get 'em; and there was a night-shirt short last week – it's got a D on it. If they send from the theatre, tell them to go to the devil; and if they want sixteen parts studied in a week, they'd better get a cast-iron actor. Yours truly, D——."

'This was a great relief to me, but it didn't seem to have soothed the stage manager much. When he recovered from his amazement, he said what he thought of the old man, which I will not repeat. There was a deuce of a row, I can tell you. Our Leading Man, who had consoled himself for being temporarily ousted from his proper position by the thought of having nothing to do all the time, and being able to go in front each night and sneer at the "star," had to take the First Old Man's place, and a pretty temper he's in about it. It's as much as one's life's worth now, even, to sneak a bit of his colour. Another old man joins us after next week, but of course that is just too late for the hard work. —— will be gone then. . .'.

CHAPTER 16

Views on Acting

QUOTE FROM two more letters, and then I have done with this stock company. The first was written just after our star had set, – or rather gone to the next town, – the second about a fortnight later:

'. . . —— left on Saturday. We had crowded houses all the time he was with us, and I'm not surprised. It must have been a treat to these benighted provincials to see real acting. No wonder country people don't care much for theatres, seeing the wretched horse-play presented to them under the name of acting. It does exasperate me to hear people talking all that thundering nonsense about the provinces being such a splendid school for young actors. Why a couple of months of it is enough to kill any idea of acting a man may have started with. Even if you had time to think of anything but how to gabble through your lines, it would be of no use. You would never be allowed to carry out any ideas of your own. If you attempted to *think*, you would be requested to look out for another shop at once. The slightest naturalness or originality would be put down to ignorance. You must walk through each part by the beaten track of rule and tradition – and such rule and tradition! The rule of Richardson's Show, the tradition of some ranting inn-yard hack. To reach the standard of dramatic art in the provinces, you have to climb down, not up. Comedy consists in having a red nose, and tumbling about the stage;

being pathetic makes you hoarse for an hour after; and as for tragedy! no one dare attempt that who hasn't the lungs of a politician.

'But —— changed all that for us. He infused a new spirit into everybody, and, when he was on the stage, the others acted better than I should ever have thought they could have done. It is the first time I have played with any one who can properly be called an actor, and it was quite a new sensation. I could myself tell that I was acting very differently to the way in which I usually act. I seemed to catch his energy and earnestness; the scene grew almost real, and I began to *feel* my part. And that is the most any one can do on the stage. As to "being the character you are representing", that is absurd. I can hardly believe in any sane person seriously putting forward such a suggestion. It is too ridiculous to argue against. Picture to yourself a whole company forgetting that they were merely acting, and all fancying themselves the people they were impersonating. Words and business would of course be out of the question. They would all say and do just what came natural to them, and just *when* it came natural; so that sometimes everybody would be talking at once, and at other times there would be nobody doing anything. Such enthusiasm as theirs would never bow to the pitiful requirements of stage illusion. They would walk over the footlights on to the heads of the orchestra, and they would lean up against the mountains in the background. It would be a grand performance, but it wouldn't last long. The police would have to be called in before the first act was over. If they were not, the Leading Man would slaughter half the other members of the company; the Juvenile Lead would run off with the Walking Lady and the property jewels; and the First Old Man would die of a broken heart. What the manager would do on the second night I don't know. If he opened at all, I suppose he would go in front and explain matters by saying:

"Ladies and gentlemen, – I must apologize for the incompleteness with which the play will be presented to you this evening. The truth is, the performance last night was so realistic all round, that there is only the Low Comedy and a General Utility left. But we've a good many corpses about the theatre, and with these, and the assistance of the two gentlemen mentioned, we will do what we can."

'Even when studying in one's own room, one cannot for a moment lose sight of one's identity. A great actor, creating a character, doesn't forget he's himself, and think he's somebody else. It's only lunatics who have those fancies. But he is a man of such vast sympathy that he can understand and enter into all human thoughts and

The Royal Court Theatre, Liverpool, 1887

feelings; and, having pictured to himself the character of the man he wishes to represent, he can follow the workings of that supposed man's mind under all possible circumstances.

'But even this sympathy must be left outside the theatre doors. Once inside, the mind must be kept clear of all distracting thoughts. What is gone through on the stage is merely an exact repetition of what is conceived in the study, and a cool head and a good memory are the only reliable servants when once the curtain is up. Of course a man should *feel* what he is acting. Feeling is the breath of acting. It is to the actor what Aphrodite's gift was to Pygmalion – it gives life to his statue. But this feeling is as much a matter of memory as the rest. The actual stage is too artificial for emotion to come to one naturally while there. Each passion is assumed and dropped by force of will, together with the words and action which accompany it. . . '.

'. . . I made a sensation here last Tuesday. I was playing the very part in which our Walking Gentleman met with his accident, and he was playing the villain, who tries to stab me while I am asleep. (The Heavy Man has left. He went soon after he had done the mischief.) Well, everything had gone very smoothly so far, and I was lying there on the couch at the back of the darkened stage, and he was leaning over me with the knife in his hand. I was quite still waiting for my cue to awake, and wondering if I could manage to start up quickly, when I raised my eyes and caught sight of R——'s face. I may have done him an injustice. His expression may have been mere acting. The whole idea was, perhaps, due to nothing but my own imagination. I have thought this since. At the time it flashed across me: "He means to revenge himself on me for having taken his place. He is going to disfigure me just as he was disfigured." In an instant I had sprung up and wrested the knife from his hand.

'We stood there looking at one another, and neither of us moved or spoke; he, livid underneath his colour, and trembling from head to foot. How long we kept in that position I do not know, for the thud of the curtain upon the stage was the first thing that recalled me to myself. Up to when I had snatched the knife from him, all had been in exact accordance with the book. After that I should have held him down by the throat, and made a speech of about eight lines. I think our impromptu tableau was more effective.

'There was immense applause, and everybody congratulated me on my success. "I suppose you know you cut out the end," said the manager; "but never mind that. I daresay you were a little nervous, and you acted splendidly, my boy."

'I didn't say it wasn't acting, and neither did R——. . . .'

I left here to join a small touring company as Juvenile Lead. I looked upon the offer as a grand opportunity at the time, and following Horace's* advice, grasped it by the forelock. I, therefore, one Sunday morning packed my basket, went round the town and shook hands with everybody – not without a pang of regret, for there are few human beings we can be with for any length of time and not be sorry to say good bye to – and then as the bright summer's sun was setting and the church bells beginning to peal, I steamed away, or rather the engine did, and the city and its people faded out of my sight, and out of my life.

Sunday is the great travelling day for actors. It loses them no time. A company can finish at one town on the Saturday night, and wake up on the Monday morning in the next, ready to get everything ship-shape for the evening. Or an actor can leave one show and join another at the other end of the kingdom without missing a single performance. I have known a man play in Cornwall on the Saturday, and at Inverness on the following Monday. But convenient though it is in this respect, in every other, Sunday travelling is most unpleasant, and, for their gratification, I can assure strict Sabbatarians that it brings with it its own punishment.

Especially to a man with a conscience – an article which, in those early days, I was unfortunate enough to possess. A conscience is a disagreeable sort of thing to have with

* Not quite sure whose advice this is. Have put it down to Horace to avoid contradiction.

one at any time. It has a nasty disposition – a cantankerous, fault finding, interfering disposition. There is nothing sociable about it. It seems to take a pleasure in making itself objectionable, and in rendering its owner as uncomfortable as possible. During these Sunday journeys, it used to vex me by every means in its power. If any mild old gentleman, sitting opposite me in the carriage, raised his eyes and looked at me, I immediately fancied he was silently reproaching me, and I felt ashamed and miserable. It never occurred to me at the time that he was every bit as bad as I was, and that I had as much right to be shocked at him as he to be horrified at me. Then I used to ask myself what my poor aunt would say if she could see me. Not that it was of the slightest consequence what the old lady would have said, but the question was just one of those petty annoyances in which a mean-spirited conscience delights. I was firmly convinced that everybody was pointing the finger of scorn at me. I don't know which particular finger is the finger of scorn: whichever it is, that, I felt, was the one that was pointed at me. At every station, my exasperating inward monitor would whisper to me: 'But for such abandoned wretches as you, all those porters and guards would be sleeping peacefully in the village church.' When the whistle sounded, my tormentor would add: 'But for you and other such despicable scoundrels, that grimy, toil-stained engine-driver would be dressed in his best clothes, lounging up against a post at his own street corner.' Such thoughts maddened me.

My fellow passengers generally let on that they were going to see sick relatives, and I would have done the same if it hadn't been for that awful basket of mine. But the inventive faculty of a newspaper reporter couldn't have explained away a basket the size of an average chest of drawers. I might have said that it contained a few delicacies for the invalid, but nobody would have believed me, and there would have been a good lie wasted.

But it is not only to people with consciences that Sunday travelling presents vexations. Even you, my dear reader, would find it unpleasant. There is a subdued going-to-a-funeral air about the whole proceeding, which makes you melancholy in spite of yourself. You miss the usual bustling attributes of railway travelling. No crowded platforms! no piles of luggage! no newspaper boys! The refreshment rooms don't seem the same places at all, and the damsels there are haughtier than ever. When you arrive at your destination, you seem to have come to a city of the dead. You pass through deserted streets to your hotel. Nobody is about. You go into the coffee-room and sit down there by yourself. After a while the boots looks in. You yearn towards him as towards a fellow creature. You would fall upon his neck and tell him all your troubles. You try to engage him in conversation, so as to detain him in the room, for you dread to be left alone again. But he doesn't enter into your feelings: he answers all questions by monosyllables, and gets away as quickly as possible. You go out for a walk. The streets are dark and silent, and you come back more miserable than you started. You order supper, but have no appetite, and cannot eat it when it comes. You retire to your room early, but cannot go to sleep. You lie there and wonder what the bill will come to, and, while thinking of this, you are softly borne away into the land of dreams, and fancy that the proprietor has asked you for a hundred and eighty-seven pounds nine and fourpence ha'penny, and that you have killed him on the spot, and left the house in your nightshirt without paying.

· CHAPTER 17 ·

I Join A 'Fit-Up'

HE SHOW WHICH I now graced with my presence was a 'fit-up.' I didn't know this beforehand, or I should never have engaged myself. A 'fit-up' is only one grade higher than a booth, which latter branch of the profession, by the way, I have always regretted never having explored. I missed the most picturesque and romantic portion of the theatrical world by not penetrating into that time-forsaken corner. Booth life is a Bohemia within a Bohemia. So far as social and artistic position is concerned, it is at the bottom of the dramatic ladder; but for interest and adventure, it stands at the very top.

Set design for a scene from *A Woman in Red*, St James's Theatre, 1868

However, I never did join a booth, so there is an end of the matter. The nearest I approached to anything of the kind was this fit-up, and that I didn't like at all. We kept to the very small towns, where there was no theatre, and fitted up an apology for a stage in any hall or room we could hire for the purpose. The town-hall was what we generally tried for, but we were not too particular; any large room did, and we would even put up with a conveniently situated barn. We carried our own props, scenery, and proscenium, and trusted for the wood-work to some local carpenter. A row of candles did duty for footlights, and a piano, hired in the town, represented the orchestra. We couldn't get a piano on one occasion, so the proprietor of the hall lent us his harmonium.

I will not linger over my experiences with this company; they were not pleasant ones. Short extracts from two letters, one written just after joining, and the other sent off just before I left, will be sufficient:

'Dear Jim, – I find I've dropped the substance and grasped the shadow (I pride myself not so much on the originality of this remark as on its applicability). I shall leave as soon as possible, and try my luck in London. My ambition to play Juvenile Lead vanished the moment I saw the Leading Lady, who is, as usual, the manager's wife. She is a fat, greasy old woman. She has dirty hands and finger nails, and perspires freely during the course of the perform-ance. She is about three times my size, and if the audiences to which we play have the slightest sense of humour – which, from what I have seen of them, I think extremely doubtful – our love-making must be a rare treat to them. How a London first-night gallery would enjoy it! I'm afraid, though, it's only wasted down here. My arm, when I try to clasp her waist, reaches to about the middle of her back; and, when we embrace, the house can't see me at all. I have to carry her half-way across the stage in one part. By Jove! I'm glad we don't play that piece often.

'She says I shall never make a good "lover" unless I throw more ardour ("*harder*", she calls it) into my acting. . . .'

'. . . Shall be with you on Monday next. Can't stand this any longer. It's ruining me. Seven-and-six was all I could get last week, and eleven shillings the week before. We are not doing bad business by any means. Indeed, we have very good houses. The old man has got the knack of making out good gag bills, and that pulls 'em in for the two or three nights we stay at each place. You know what I mean by a "gag" bill: "The Ruined Mill by Dead Man's Pool. Grace Mervin thinks to meet a friend, but finds a foe. Harry Baddun recalls old days. 'Why do you not love me?' 'Because you are a bad man.' 'Then die!' The struggle on the brink!! 'Help!!' 'There is none to help you here.' 'You lie, Harry Baddun; *I* am here.' A hand from the grave!! Harry Baddun meets his doom!!!"

'That's what I mean by a gag bill.

'Whatever money is made, however, he takes care to keep for himself. He can always put up at the best hotel in the place, while we have to pawn our things to pay for the meanest of lodgings.

'It isn't only actors who get robbed by these managers: authors also suffer pretty considerably. We have two copyright pieces in our list, both of which draw very well, but not a penny is paid for performing them. To avoid any chance of unpleasantness, the titles of the pieces and the names of the chief characters are altered. So that even if the author or his friends (supposing it possible for an author to have any friends) were on the lookout, they would never know anything about it. And, if they did, it would be of no use. It would be throwing good money after bad to attempt to enforce payment from the men who do this sort of thing, – and I hear that it is done all over the provinces, they have no money, and none can be got out of them. Your penniless man can comfortably defy half the laws in the statute book.

'What a nuisance firearms are on the stage! I thought I was blinded the other night, and my eyes are painful even now. The fellow should have fired up in the air. It is the only safe rule on a small stage, though it does look highly ridiculous to see a man drop down dead because another man fires a pistol at the moon. But there is always some mishap with them. They either don't go off at all, or else they go off in the wrong place, and, when they do go off there is generally an accident. They can never be depended upon. You rush on to the stage, present a pistol at somebody's head, and say, "Die!" but the pistol only goes click, and the man doesn't know whether to die or not. He waits while you have another try at him, and the thing clicks again; and then you find out that the property man hasn't put a cap on it, and you turn round to get one. But the other man, thinking it is all over, makes up his mind to die at once from nothing else but fright, and, when you come back to kill him for the last time, you find he's already dead.

'We have recourse to some rum makeshifts here, to eke out our wardrobes. My old frock coat, with a little cloth cape which one of the girls has cut out for me pinned on underneath the collar, and with a bit of lace round the cuffs, does for the gallant of half the old comedies; and, when I pin the front corners back and cover them with red calico, I'm a French soldier. A pair of white thingumies does admirably for buckskin riding breeches, and, for the part of a Spanish conspirator, I generally borrow my landlady's tablecloth. . . .'

It was about the end of October when I found myself once more in London. The first thing I then did was to go to my old shop on the Surrey-side. Another company and another manager were there, but the latter knew me, and, as I owned a dress suit, engaged me at a salary of twelve shillings weekly to play the part of a swell. When I had been there just one week, he closed. Whether it was paying me that twelve shillings that broke him I cannot say; but on Monday morning some men came and cut the gas off, and then he said he shouldn't go on any longer, and that we must all do the best we could for ourselves.

I, with two or three others, thereupon started off for a theatre at the East End, which was about to be opened for a limited number of nights by some great world-renowned actor. This was about the fortieth world-renowned party I had heard of for the first time within the last twelvemonth. My education in the matter of world-renowned people had evidently been shamefully neglected.

The theatre was cunningly contrived, so that one had to pass through the bar of the adjoining public-house – to the landlord of which it belonged – to get to the stage. Our little party was saved from temptation, however, for I don't think we could have mustered a shilling amongst the lot of us that morning. I was getting most seriously hard up at this time. The few pounds I had had left, after purchasing my wardrobe and paying my railway fares, etc., had now dwindled down to shillings, and unless things mended, I felt I should have to throw up the sponge and retire from the stage. I was determined not to do this though, till the very last, for I dreaded the chorus of 'I told you so's,' and 'I knew very well how 'twould be's,' and such like well-known and exasperating crows of triumph, with which, in these cases, our delighted friends glorify themselves and crush us.

The East End theatre proved a stop-gap for a while. I was fortunate enough to be one of those engaged out of the crowd of eager and anxious applicants, among whom I met a couple from the fit-up company I had lately left, they having come to the same conclusion as myself, viz., that it was impossible to live well and 'dress respectably on and off the stage' upon an average salary of ten shillings weekly. The engagement was only for a fortnight, and there is only one incident connected with it that I particularly remember. That was my being 'guyed' on one occasion. We were playing a melodrama, the scene of which was laid in some outlandish place or other, and the stage manager insisted on my wearing a most outrageous costume. I knew it would be laughed at, especially in that neighbourhood, and my expectations were more than fulfilled. I hadn't been on the stage five seconds before I heard a voice from the gallery hoarsely inquire: 'What is it, Bill?' And then another voice added: 'Tell us what it is, and you shall have it.'

A good deal of laughter followed these speeches. I got hot all over, and felt exceedingly uncomfortable and nervous. It was as much as I could do to recollect my part, and it was with a great effort that I began my first line. No sooner had I opened my mouth, however, than somebody in the pit exclaimed, in tones of the utmost surprise, 'Blowed if it ain't alive!'

After that, the remarks on my personal appearance fell thick and fast: 'Look well in a shop window, that bloke!' 'Nice suit to take your gal out on a Sunday in!' 'This style, thirty shillin's,' etc.; while one good-natured man sought to put me at ease by roaring out in a stentorian voice, 'Never you mind, old man; you go on. They're jealous 'cos you've got nice clothes on.' How I managed to get through the part I don't know. I became more nervous and awkward every minute, and, of course, the more I bungled, the more the house jeered. I gained a good deal of sympathy behind, for most of them had had similar experiences of their own; but I was most intensely miserable all that evening, and, for the next night or two, quite dreaded to face the audience. Making game of any one is a very amusing occupation, but the 'game' doesn't see the fun till a long while afterwards. I can't bear to hear any of the performers chaffed when I'm at a theatre. Actors are necessarily a sensitive class of people, and I don't think those who make fun of them, when any little thing goes wrong, have any idea of the pain they are inflicting. It is quite right, and quite necessary sometimes, that disapprobation should be expressed, and that unmistakably, but it should be for the purpose of correcting real faults. 'Guying' is, as a rule, indulged in only by the silliest portion of the audience, and for no other object but to display their own vulgar wit.

After my fortnight at the East End, I went as one of the chorus in a new opera-bouffe to be brought out at a West-End theatre. We rehearsed for three weeks, the piece ran for one, and then I again took a provincial engagement, which, as it was now close upon Christmas, was easy enough to obtain.

My stay in London had not been very profitable to me, but it had given my friends a treat, as they had been able to come and see me act again. At least, I suppose it was a treat to them, though they did not say so. My friends are always most careful never to overdo the thing in the matter of praise. I cannot accuse them of sycophancy. They scorn to say pleasant things that they don't mean. They prefer saying unpleasant things that they do mean. There's no humbug about them; they never hesitate to tell me just exactly what they think of me. This is good of them. I respect them for saying what they think; but if they would think a little differently, I should respect them still more. I wonder if everybody's friends are as conscientious? I've heard of people having 'admiring friends,' and 'flattering friends,' and 'over-indulgent friends,' but I've never had any of that sort myself. I've often thought I should rather like to, though, and if any gentleman has more friends of that kind than he wants, and would care to have a few of the opposite stamp, I am quite ready to swop with him. I can warrant mine never to admire or flatter under any circumstances whatsoever; neither will he find them over-indulgent. To a man who really wishes to be told of his faults, they would be invaluable; on this point they are candour itself. A conceited man would also derive much benefit from their society. I have myself.

· CHAPTER *18* ·

My Last Appearance

I LEFT LONDON exactly twelve months from the day on which I had started to fulfil my first provincial engagement, and I did not return to it again while I was an actor. I left it with my baggage early in the morning by the newspaper express from Euston; I returned to it late at night, footsore and hungry, and with no other possessions than the clothes I stood upright in.

Of the last few months of my professional life, the following brief extracts will speak. A slightly bitter tone runs through some of them, but at the time they were written I was suffering great disappointment, and everything was going wrong with me – circumstances under which a man is perhaps apt to look upon his surroundings through smoke-coloured glasses.

Three weeks after Christmas I write:

'. . . Business good and money regular. Business is almost always good, though, at pantomime time: the test will come later on, when we begin to travel. How a provincial audience does love a pantomime! and how I do hate it! I can't say I think very highly of provincial audiences. They need a lot of education in art. They roar over coarse buffoonery, and applaud noisy rant to the echo. One might as well go to Billingsgate to study English as to the provinces to learn acting.

'I played First Low Comedy on Saturday night at half an hour's notice, the real First Low Comedy being hopelessly intoxicated at the time. It's a pity, amidst all the talk about the elevation of the stage, that the elevation of actors is not a less frequent occurrence. It can hardly improve the reputation of the profession in the eyes of the public, when they take up the *Era* and read advertisement after advertisement,

The Theatre of Marvels

ending with such lines as, "None but sober people need apply." "Must contrive to keep sober, at all events during the performance." "People who are constantly getting drunk need not write." I've known some idiots actually make themselves half tipsy on purpose before coming on the stage, evidently thinking, because they can't act when they've got all their few wits about them, that they'll manage better if they get rid of them altogether. There is a host of wonderful traditions floating about the theatrical world of this, that, and the other great actor having always played this, that, and the other part while drunk; and so, when some wretched little actor has to take one of these parts, he, fired by a noble determination to follow in the footsteps of his famous predecessor, gets drunk too.

'Bad language is another thing that the profession might spare a lot of, and still have enough remaining for all ordinary purposes. I remember one night at —— we all agreed to fine ourselves a penny each time we swore. We gave it up after two hours' trial: none of us had any money left. . . .'

Six weeks later:

'. . . Business gets worse instead of better. Our manager has behaved very well indeed. He paid us our salaries right up to the end of last week, though any one could see he was losing money every night: and then on Saturday, after treasury, he called us all together, and put the case frankly. He said he could not continue as he had been doing, but that, if we liked, he was ready to keep on with us for a week or two longer upon sharing terms, to see if the luck turned. We agreed to this, and so formed ourselves into what is called a "commonwealth" – though common poverty would be a more correct term in my opinion, for the shares each night, after deducting expenses, have been about eighteenpence. The manager takes three of these shares (one for being manager, one for acting, and the other one to make up the three), and the rest of us have one each. I'm getting awfully hard up, though I live for a week, now, on less than what I've often given for a dinner. . . .'

A week later, this company broke up, and I then joined another that was close handy at the time. It is from this latter that the following is written:

'. . . I just manage to keep my head above water, and that is all. If things get worse, I shall be done for. I've no money of my own left now.
'A very sad thing happened here last week. Our leading man died suddenly from heart disease, leaving his wife and two children totally destitute. If he had been a big London actor, for half his life in receipt of a salary of, say, three thousand a year, the theatrical press would have teemed with piteous appeals to the public, all his friends would have written to the papers generously offering to receive subscriptions on his behalf, and all the theatres would have given performances at double prices to help pay his debts and funeral expenses. As, however, he had never earned anything higher than about two pounds a week, Charity could hardly be expected to interest herself about the case; and so the wife supports herself and her children by taking in washing. Not that I believe she would ask for alms, even were there any chance of

her getting them, for, when the idea was only suggested to her, she quite fired up, and talked some absurd nonsense, about having too much respect for her husband's profession to degrade it into a mere excuse for begging. . . .'

This company also went wrong. It was a terrible year for theatres. Trade was bad everywhere, and 'amusements' was the very first item that people with diminishing incomes struck out of the list of their expenditure. One by one I parted with every valuable I had about me, and a visit to the pawnshop, just before leaving each town, became as essential as packing. I went through the country like a distressed ship through troubled waters, marking my track by the riches I cast overboard to save myself. My watch I left behind me in one town, my chain in another; a ring here, my dress suit there; a writing-case I dropped at this place, and a pencil case at that. And so things went on – or rather, off – till the beginning of May, when this letter, the last of the series, was written:

'Dear Jim, – Hurrah! I've struck oil at last. I think it was time I did after what I've gone through. I was afraid the profession would have to do without me, but it's all safe now. I'm in a new company – joined last Saturday, and we're doing splendidly. Manager is a magnificent fellow, and a good man of business. He understands how to make the donkey go. He advertises and bills right and left, spares no expense, and does the thing thoroughly well. He's a jolly nice fellow, too, and evidently a man of intelligence, for he appreciates me. He engaged me without my applying to him at all, after seeing me act one night last week, when he was getting his company together. I play First Walking Gent. at thirty-five shillings a week. He has been a captain in the army, and is a thorough gentleman. He never bullies or interferes, and everybody likes him. He is going all round the North of England, taking all the big Lancashire and Yorkshire towns, and then going to bring us to London for the winter. He wants me to sign an agreement for one year certain at two pounds five. I haven't appeared to be too anxious. It's always best to hang back a bit in such cases, so I told him I would think it over; but of course I shall accept. Can't write any more now. I'm just off to dine with him. We stop here three weeks, and then go to——. Very comfortable lodgings.
Yours, ——.'

· ON THE STAGE – AND OFF ·

That was written on Tuesday. On Saturday, we came to the theatre at twelve for treasury. The Captain was not there. He had gone that morning to pay a visit to Sir somebody or other, one of the neighbouring gentry, who was a great friend of his, and he had not yet returned. He would be back by the evening – so the courteous acting manager assured us – and treasury would take place after the performance.

So in the evening, when the performance was over, we all assembled on the stage and waited. We waited about ten minutes, and then our Heavy Man, who had gone across the way to get a glass before they shut up, came back with a scared face to say that he'd just seen the booking-clerk from the station, who had told him that the 'Captain' had left for London by an early train that morning. And no sooner had the Heavy Man made this announcement, than it occurred to the call-boy that he had seen the courteous acting manager leave the theatre immediately after the play had begun, carrying a small black bag.

I went back to the dressing-room, gathered my things into a bundle, and came down again with it. The others were standing about the stage, talking low, with a weary, listless air. I passed through them without a word, and reached the stage door. It was one of those doors that shut with a spring. I pulled it open, and held it back with my foot, while I stood there on the threshold for a moment, looking out at the night. Then I turned my coat collar up, and stepped into the street: the stage door closed behind me with a bang and a click, and I have never opened another one since.